The Devil Dog Road by Mr. Mo

-masturbation & pornography-
OVERCOMING SEXUAL ADDICTION

By
Barnabus Fuller

Bloomington, IN

authorHOUSE™

Milton Keynes, UK

AuthorHouse™
1663 Liberty Drive, Suite 200
Bloomington, IN 47403
www.authorhouse.com
Phone: 1-800-839-8640

AuthorHouse™ UK Ltd.
500 Avebury Boulevard
Central Milton Keynes, MK9 2BE
www.authorhouse.co.uk
Phone: 08001974150

First published by AuthorHouse 2/03/2006

ISBN: 1-4208-9189-8 (sc)

Printed in the United States of America
Bloomington, Indiana

This book is printed on acid-free paper.

Preface

This is a journey of a real person, although somewhat embellished, on the road to becoming potentially a dirty old man. The road travels through pre-puberty sexual encounters, puberty itself disciplined by a celibate and chaste lifestyle and the post puberty reacting against the adolescent chastity disciplines embraced as a Roman Catholic Seminarian.

If that isn't enough, the memoir thinly disguised as hard-core porn, has a moralizing agenda that combines philosophy, psychology and theology to create a counterpoint as off beat, yet persuasive as the "beat" writings of a Jack Kerouac.

Sex, sexuality, abuse and boundaries are recognized, reflected upon and decisions made through the understanding of these phenomenal and powerful energies.

Uniquely, I've especially tried to address conflicted, guilty Roman Catholic males who still masturbate and think they are sinning. Most have not a problem with birth control or the idea that anything goes with one's spouse; but the jacking the Johnson still disturbs them from a Catholic moral point of view, which says it is an intrinsic evil and a grave moral disorder. (Catechism of the Catholic Church article 2352 et al.)

I really have no answer here, except I offer my worldview of *both/and* rather than an *either/or* approach.

Most will agree that using sexual functions outside of marriage, outside of its purpose of expressing mutual love and possible procreation and using sex for solitary pleasure is suspect. Innately, there seems to be more to it than sticky fingers.

The book is divided into three parts:

Memoir Narrative.

Carnal Stream of Consciousness as the Intermezzo

A Play

This is a book based on a worldview and philosophy of "both/and" rather than "either/or". It is in fact both a journey of the earthy and the spiritual, intermixed and interrelated. It is hoped it will be a blessing to both body and soul, and also fun to read.

"Nothing is good or bad but thinking makes it so." William Shakespear

TO
ST. BARNABAS

THE ENCOURAGER

He encouraged all to stand firm in their commitment to the Lord.

When Barnabas arrived at Antioch and saw God's grace work there, he rejoiced, for he was a good man, filled with the Holy Spirit and with Faith.

It was at Antioch that the believers were first called Christians.

(Acts 11:23-26)

Forward

At first glance, this book may appear as hardcore pornography written by an immature bisexual.

The middle section entitled *Intermezzo* both graphically titillates and yet leaves a residue of discontent with solitary sexual addiction.

A recovering addict to masturbation and pornography writes it.

As young man, I relate adventures of US Navy awakening to varied sexual experiences. Post marriage reflections and a stretch of 20 years of fidelity are followed by the crash of divorce and incipient homosexual desires. The finding of a soul-mate and the eventual process and journey of recovering true integrity as vintage years approach complete the story.

Table of Contents

PART 1: THE EARLY YEARS   1

Transitions   12

Early Seminary Days at St. Nazianz   17

Rule of the Day   19

Summer Days While On Vacation   22

Mater Christi, the New Seminary   24

In Between, Before the Rock   26

The Rock   27

Home for the Holidays, and then Some   29

The Navy   33

I'm in the Navy Now   36

Europe and the Med   41

Back to the Good Ol' USA and D.C.   45

Westward Ho   48

Where is all this going?   51

The Other Job: Computers   52

Breakout   54

Back to Sales   55

PART 2: MASTURBATION AND PORNOGRAPHY

59

Introduction 61

The Gatorade Bottle and the Carrot 62

The Seminary-Early Years, A Follow-on Reflection on Part I 66

Viginity and Booze 69

Drinking Re-evaluated 74

Update on the Drinking Deal, or Ordeal: 76

The Used Rubber in the Bathroom Wastebasket 78

And there was being 79

Masturbation 80

XXX 83

Dress Fit to Kill 85

Was Boredom the Culprit? 88

What is the difference between LOVE and LUST? 90

Paper Dolls 91

Letting Go 93

Mistaken Identity 95

The Homosexual 98

Did Jesus Masturbate? 101

Dirty Jokes 104

Movies, Past and Present 105

Pederasty, Why does it Sound so Nasty? 108

Centerfold 109

Grace 113

The Action of Grace 118

Gays, Aids and Structures 120

The Orgasmic Bible 122

Slavery or Liberation? 123

PART 3: ...ON THE ROAD AGAIN 127

Divorce and a Book of 25 Cancelled Chicks 129

Along Comes Maria 133

Changes, Back West Again and Then Some 135

The Odysseys 135

Priestly Desires 140

Daytona Bike Week 142

PART 4: CHANGES, TRANSITIONS AND RADICAL RE-INVOLVEMENT 145

POSTSCRIPT: WET 153

The Devil Dog Road Part 1

By Mister Mo

The year was 1938. My mother lay in agony in upper state New York about to release from her hugeness a newborn son. His name is to be "Mo".

Mo took a peek and said "Man, here I come!" He leaped out of the vaginal canal feet first, and the only difficulty experience was his shades, his Oakley sunglasses, hung up just abit. "Man, the light of the overhead was just too bright to be without them!"

The doctor remarked that I was so ugly, he slapped my mother twice.

Having drawn my first breath of air, I let out a whopping cry of "I'm here, bend one buddy."

How in the world did I get the name of "Mo"? It seems dear Mom, when laying in the delivery room was chanting a Zen mantra of "Oma, Omah, Oma." At which time Dad came in a little bit prepped with the blackness of Jack Daniels, and misunderstood Mom's chanting as a response to his question: "Ah, dear, whatisname gonna be?" Hence, a clearly defined name of Mo.

There's a lot of dignity to this appellation. Remember Tibbs in The Heat of the Night? When the sheriff, Rod Steiger, asked what he should call Sidney Poitier? Poitier emphatically stated: "Call me

MR. TIBBS!" To enhance my stature further in the world, call me MR. MO.

Of course, this demand was not realized at the first diaper change. My father realized that diaper changing was a life changing experience, especially when he found out that poop doesn't come out saran wrapped.

"Mo, you wait here while I get your mother."

This could have been the beginning of a sh..ty life, however, although I need help in cleaning up my act, I started anew, clean, washed, and smiling.

My Mom, a good Catholic, wrapped my in a frilly white outfit and whisked me before a priest in a rather cold church. It was December and the heat was what little steam came out of a very remote radiator. But the water in the Baptismal fount was not too cold once the ice had been chopped through.

"In the name of the Father, and of the Son and of the Holy Ghost..." I'm signed on as a Roman Catholic.

PART 1: THE EARLY YEARS

Dad was in the ArmyAirCorps and fighting JAPS in a remote island off Australia. Mother and my older brother Ralph stayed with the grandparents.

Grandpa was retired from building locomotives. He was a skilled machinist, even though he never learned to read. An affable gent who in his younger days rode a gear driven bicycle with toe clips. He never learned to drive a car. The bike was really unique and when I was able to ride my Hawthorne (J.C. Higgins manufacture) without crashing, I managed to strip the gears on Grandpa's bike and render it a place in the basement as a permanent shroud.

Before a two-wheeler, I was a trike kind of guy and hung out with Janice and Myra. Janice was a kind of sexy five year old who suggested she would show me hers if I would show her mine. We journey behind Gramps workshop and dropped trou to her hiking up skirt. Bloody marvelous! The start of grand and glorious sexual discovery and adventure.

Years later when I visited Janice while at home during vacation from the seminary she enthralled me with Lucky Strikes and tales of high school social life of which my background celibate seminary training left me in a daze. On an earlier visit before my journey to the seminary, Janice and Myra peeked my interest with discussions of having their first period.

All this of course was jumped started in second grade by a girl named Barbara and her invitation to go after school to her house to play spin-the-bottle. Actual kissing techniques were to be improved, but this was a great start.

Years and years later, my first real kiss was with a passionate Italian girl who wanted to show me how it was done. She was a total tonsil sucking French kissing extravagance, whose tongue reached and penetrated my brain forever. Oh Maria, we will meet you later.

Now, dear reader, you may think that I am and was and will be a consummate young stud evolving into a walking hard-on with absolutely no dick management and whose future lies in becoming a dirty old man. Perhaps.

Life with Grandparents changed when the WWII ended and Dad came marching home. We had a little relocation to the South where I went barefoot to school and helped make homemade potato chips with Audry.

Audry was a cute little South Carolina girl who disdained underwear. When we sat on the porch eating chips, she didn't cross her legs.

Although Audry was neat, my attention was drawn to a fig tree upon which where very ripe figs upon which June bugs feasted. It's easy to catch a J-bug when its head is buried in a fig. Did Audry resemble a fig? I captured a bug and tied a piece of threat to it and launched it into space. What a grand flight, buzzing around, ecologically sound, no pollution, just experiencing the thrill of controlled flight.

Not all the Southern experiences were as soaring. Old Lady MaZeke next door was a dour maid who like to poison cats...ours being one of them. The only reprise was to make a sulfur stink bomb with my brother Ralph's chemistry set and plop through her window. Whew, I'm surprised it didn't burn the house down. I think MaZeke did get even though, but we could never prove who tied a dead skunk to the radiator of our '41 Chevy. Whew and pew, the smell never left that car.

Back north to Long Island and the Second Grade Barbara incident, I was seven at the time and about the only remembrances were about Ralph showing movies on an 16mm projector, black and white cartoons. He charged the neighborhood kids a nickel.

I do remember going to a high school football game one Saturday afternoon. I snuck in over the fence and was caught by a security guard. He took me to a little cabin just off the football field and said he was going to call my parents. He gave me a choice and said he wouldn't do it if I let him suck me off. I'm not sure what he meant, and since I didn't see any phone, I thought I'd make a break for it. He already had his pants around his ankles and was lowering his briefs, so he wasn't in much of a position to chase me. I wonder what would have happen to this seven year old boy if something did happen that day.

Third grade found us back in the Tri-City area of New York. Romance springs anew in the hopeful embrace of Cathy. I fell hopelessly in love at her eighth birthday party. She was bending over to bob for apples and her short skirt hiked up to reveal cotton panties with little butterflies. Is Cathy like Audry, like a fig. I had to settle for eating an apple, just like Adam?

You know I went through thirteen different schools in eight years. Fifth grade I had my first real almost life threatening fight. There was this King of the Hill named Hershkowiz and his morbid sidekick and zombie, Graham. There delight was to try out new punches on me on a daily basis.

I asked Dad to show me how to defend myself and he taught me the"ol' one two". This is a boxing maneuver where one feigns with a left and delivers a blow to the stomach with the right hand, delivering another blow with the left to the nose. If the assailant grabs his nose, hit him again in the stomach. If he grabs his stomach, hit him in the nose.

Actually, this is not a bad legitimate move, but, I would have been better off, kicking him in the nuts.

The next day, Hershy steps on my foot and says, "what are you goin' to do 'bout it?" The Zombie Graham is standing nearby chuckling. I set up, and feign with my left and forget all my training by deliver a wimpy tap on Hershy's cheek. After he recovered his surprise, he adjusted his skull and cross bones ring with the red ruby eyes and smacked me in the forehead leaving the ring's impression. I turned red and kept from crying. Hersy said he will kill me after school.

Just outside Oneida Jr. High, the fifth grade gathers to see my demise. Graham is designated by Hersy to put me away. My old friend Willy McCain had shown me a neat choke hold kind of thing and I grabbed Graham and began choking him. He turned blue.

Begged for mercy, "I give up!" It felt too good I continued. Hersey was amazed. I let Graham go and Hersy and I became good friends ever after.

Fifth grade continued my interest in girls, one in particular whose name was Jackie. I manage a stealth attack and got a kiss. I heard that Jackie like to f-ck. Never found out about that, but was interested to find out more.

We had a great Irish/English setter named Pal. These were the days when dogs ran loose, pooped where they wanted; spend time barking, liking balls and rear ends and generally getting laid whenever there was a willing doggess. Much like today's non-dick manager kind of guy.

Pal stepped on some glass and cut his paw. Dad bandaged him up and nursed him back to health. A really good Dad. Poor ol' Pal like to chase cars and finally lost.

Dad's new duty station took him to Denver. Oh what a delight, Denver in the 50's. And the girls! Now in Seventh grade, we studied in particular cute bottoms and panties going up the stairs. One in particular, her name was Margie, had a nice bosom and the challenge was to "cop a feel". I came close, but chickened out.

Roger and Dwayne where the ringleaders in sexual exploits, real or imagined. Dwayne would tell of his Saturday trips to see Barbara and get laid. He like to bring alcohol to school in glass vials and mostly he was stoned. He was jacking off in shop class in the utility room and wanted to know if there were any volunteers. Gilbert, who likes to grab other boy's genitals quickly responded. Mr. Watt, the shop teacher may have caught them, I don't know.

Roger's big interest was getting a boner in class and pointing to his tenting Levis. He was a latch key kid and one day invited me to his apartment. He showed me his cum spots on the bathroom wall, where he jacked off from the edge of the bathtub. Quite a shot. He offered a demonstration, but I left.

My first jacking experience was quite natural as I played with myself in the shower. No one had shown me, it was just a natural thing. I was amazed at how pleasant it was and of the white boy cum that happened. I don't know why I felt guilty as I repeated beating off in the bedroom and on the john. But I did.

My friend Ted came over one day and I showed him a rubber; I think it was a Sheik. I don't remember where I got it; think I may have found it. I always got the hots when I found used rubbers, you know, just the rings. Anyway I asked him if he wanted to try it on and he went into the bathroom and did so. He rolled it up as it was before and gave it back to me, said it was neato.

Dad had purchased a 1949 black Pontiac Chieftain right off the show room floor. It was fully loaded: sun visor, clock, radio, Hydromantic and a straight eight engine. We took a trip to California from Denver to see some of the folk's old friends and see the sights.

We stopped for gas, Dad had a 5 cent Coke and I wandered in the Curio shop. After experimenting with genuine rattlesnake eggs (a brown envelope with a wounded rubber band thingy that vibrated when you opened the envelop causing me to jump a mile), I found a brochure with various breasts sizes and descriptions drawn in a cartoon manner. I found this very instructive and bought it. I liked

looking at it and feeling my bone grow. Didn't quite understand it but thought it nasty and nice.

We journeyed to Hollywood, Beverly Hills etc. and to the home of my parents' friends, among which was thirteen year old Maggie. Maggie was a true California beach girl, right out of Bay watch. I mean she had hooters. I studied my Curio shop brochure and identified shape, size and name. She must have caught me starring and thought I was more mature than my 10 year old puberty revealed. She started hitting on me. Lord, what would have happened if I lost my virginity at 10? Actually, I was a virgin until twenty-three, Lord, amazing but true.

We returned to Denver with my brochure and virginity still intact. One of my buddies in seventh grade had a mantra: "Jizz, the best nickel drink there is!" He was a pimply faced grinning kind of kid who fantasized getting laid every moment of consciousness.

I cut lawns with my brother Ralph who compensated me 50 cents a lawn. In Denver, the lawns were close together and just really fragrant and green. The smell of cut grass was a great way to start an early summer day.

Having acquired $13.50 all in quarters, dimes and nickels, I was ready to buy my OK Cub .049 gas model airplane engine. What a neat device, it fired by means of a glow plug, neat smelling methane fuel and a mighty whack of the forefinger.

I built a control line balsa wood plane and Ted and I went to Golden Park to fly it. Crap, first try I controlled it into a tree. Ted saw the end of flying and peddled on home. I was picking up the pieces when an older guy knelt down beside me. Funny, he was wearing a brown suit, tie etc. and seemed concerned that I was not

particularly joyful. He patted my knee and said he could make me happy and feel better. He then said we could go behind the bushes and he would suck me off. "All the boys really like it" he said.

I peddled after Ted quickly and wondered what would have happened to this ten year old, seventh grade boy if that brown suit took me into the bushes.

The thought of someone sucking my cock stirred me up. I thought of sucking Ted's cock and Ted sucking my cock. I also thought about taking down his pants and briefs and rubbing my cock on his crack. I even thought about f-cking him in the ass. These images would carry with me, like, always. I never have experienced my Johnson sliding up and penetrating a bud, an anus, and experiencing the gripping and releasing of a man's or boy's spincter muscles as I hurried to the prostate and filled the crack with white, creamy cum.

Dad's duty station ended all too soon and we were off again to stay with the grandparents while Dad reported to St. John's Newfoundland.

I entered yet another Junior High.School and turning eleven I was even more interested in the ladies. *Blue Moon* and *Harbor Lights* were the melodies for the gym dances with the girls in pleated skirts and white rolled down socks with loafers. Many bosomed out just dying for some one to cop a feel, or so I thought.. One in particular was noted for her graciousness; Debra who all the boys thought liked it. I was able to arrange a seat next to her at the Central movie house and sat with sweaty palms, just itching to cop one. Didn't, darn it.

I rather enjoyed our short stay at Gram's. I was able to steal some Camels from Gramp and sneak smokes while building another airplane up in my secluded attic room. Neat room, although some nights I would hear Gramp going after some with Gram with a lot of snorting and such. The bed really squeaked.

Transitions

Newfoundland is a very hostile, desolate island and produces like people. The Newfies are made fun of almost universally. They hardly speak the language, pay too much for booze and cigarettes, have bad teeth and live mostly in hovels.

Not being a heavy smoker, I like *Herbert Tarrytons*. Before coming to Newfoundland, I occasionally would put a quarter into a vending machine and get a pack of *Pall Mall*. A delicious non-filtered ciggie in a red pack which state *"In Signo Vincit"*, Latin for "In this sign you will conquer." All twenty-five cents would buy you in Nfld would be ciggies three cents each or two for five cents. *Black Cat, Gems, Sweet Caporal, Senior Service* and *Players* just to name a few of the broken packs of ciggies in the little store front markets that housed the owner and others upstairs. Another store front treat were toffees. Quite delicious, but really stuck to your teeth.

My buddy took me fishing in Newfie manner which was to wade in a stream and feel under rocks for trout. Once having felt one, the fish would squirm and thrash about until suitable pressure was brought to bear by crushing said fish to the underside of the rock until limpness occurred. We would then throw the gasping fish into a pail. I brought several home and threw them into a well in the backyard. Funny thing, during the winter the well would freeze solid; it was only three feet deep and not really a water supply for the house. Come springtime and the thaw, the trout were alive

and well? Hmmmm, how did they do that? They must have been frozen solid at one time.

School was definitely a horror. The Christian Brothers thought education was rote memory and writing memorized answers in blue newsprint booklets. During the winter, the classroom windows were left open and we all wore coats in class. Brother explained to me this was to keep everyone awake. Some still dozed off and were administered the leather strap. The brothers had two varieties, one long for butt whacking and one short for hand searing. Ouch!

One charming Newfie decided that he didn't like my looks or speech and said he would split my head open with a rock as soon as we got out of school. Shades of Graham and Herskowitz.. Rather than try the ol' one-two, or the choke hold, I said, "Hey, watch out!" and pointed behind him. As he turned I kick him in the crotch as hard as I could. So hard, in fact, I feel over backwards. Fortunately, my kick connected and down he went with a cry of unbelievable volume and cursing. That established me as a dude not to be reckoned with.

I did have a sorta friend in Clifford. He was a jovial, slovenly lad who always seemed to have a partial ciggie butt to share and tall stories about his conquests. He asked me one day if I would like to meet his girl friend who would like to be screwed by both of us. I wasn't to sure about all this but said "OK." Nothing happened; we went for fish and chips. She was six years old. She looked older because she smoked and drank rum and coke.

Rum and coke was the favorite Newfie beverage regardless of age, especially *Lemon Hart Demara* rum. Black, strong, and delicious. This went well with the *Bull Durham* roll your own ciggies, or

perhaps a better blend of *Target* tobacco if we could afford it. The *Bull Durham* could be had at the PX on the base for one cent a pack including papers.

There was a tempting female named Hilary. We went on some airbase sponsored bus trip to the "beach." The beaches in Nfld are strictly for ship wrecks and seals, nothing but rocks and icy cold surf. Steep cliffs limited trespass and also the fact that out houses were perched on the cliffs so that instead of flushing, the stuff just rolled down the bank to the sea.

We arrived at our destination and Hilary stuck her toe in and I followed. We both turned blue and decided to head back to the warmth of the bus. As we approached we heard a rustling along side the wooded path and saw our bus driver mightily banging one of the girls from the base. Hilary wanted a better look. She was in a white one piece swim suit and looked mighty fetching. We went back to the bus and no one was there so we settled down and put a blanket over us. I reached down between her thighs and put my finger on her warm "V." It was a heavenly soft fuzzy sensation. I so wanted to press into her now moistening slit, but we heard approaching kids and quit. I had a lot of dreams about that one piece bathing suit and Hilary.

I was still jacking off but still felt guilty about it. The school, St. Pat's, had a retreat. I picked up a Catholic Missal, Fr. Steadman's Sunday Mass, and read some Gospel passages. I felt drawn to the Lord and went to confession. The priest was a gentle soul, but schooled in old time moral theology. On that basis he asked me how many times and if I had an "emission of seed?"

I pretty much gave up my mortal sins of beating off and became interested in becoming an altar boy at the base chapel. To my knowledge, this was in the early 50's, priests were not diddling young boys to any great extent. The chaplain here was exemplary, and no bad habits other than probable excessive drinking and smoking at the Officer's Club.

He taught be the Latin responses: *"Ad Deum qui Laetificat, Juventutum meum."* I will go to the altar of God, the joy of my youth.

This started me on my road to the priesthood. I really did not like Nfld and wanted to get out of there. Also, I started going to mass at St. Bonnaventure Cathedral and enjoying the mysticism, incense, smell of candles and the shadowy spirituality. I purchased a missal printed in Belgium and bound in leather for five dollars and had it blessed by the resident Bishop. I wrote in the inside cover "Blessed by a Bishop", but later removed the inscription because I thought it showy-offy.

I talked to Mom and said I thought I would like to be a priest. She talked to the base chaplain, Fr. McDevers, who said he knew of a high school seminary ninety miles north of Milwaukee Wisconsin, and would write them for information and application. Well, this was fine, because Mom's sister, Bea, lived in Milwaukee and could keep an eye on things. So, the Seminary, a Religious order, said they would be glad to enroll me, the cost would be $600 a year for room, board and tuition.

Dad packed a footlocker with all my clothes for all seasons, linens and towel, the works. He was superb packer. Mom had to sew my laundry number on every article, she was a superb sewer- onner.

15

So, at thirteen years of age Dad and I boarded a MATS (Military Air Transport Service) DC9 and took off for Westover Air Force Base. From there I journeyed by myself by train to Chicago where I was met by Chris and Uncle Bob. While sitting in the car while Uncle was running an errand, some one clipped us. I noted the license plate of the car that hit us and gave it to Bob. I didn't have a pencil so I punched out the number with a pin on a piece of paper; worked pretty good.

Early Seminary Days at St. Nazianz

I arrived with footlocker and a bag of homemade chocolate chips from Aunt Bea at the steps of Salvatorian Seminary, St. Nazianz, Wisconsin. St. Nazianz is 90 miles north of Milwaukee, and is unremarkable by being unnoticed by a cross roads which comprises the town.

Salvatorian Seminary is a high school and first two years of college known as a Minor Seminary. This type of institution is virtually unknown today, but in the 1950's they thrived and numbered over 30,000 seminarians in the United States.

Fr. Maurice gave me a tour and helped me get settled. My new home consisted of a metal locker, a bed, night stand, and desk in the study hall. It's surprising how little one needs.

Other freshman arrived and we are now a class of about 30 9th grade students. Our typical dress consisted of wash type pants, shirt, a cover shirt or jacket and tie. I grew a lot in my first year and all my pants became high-water, as did my shirt sleeves. Also, I didn't have a good warm coat for the coming winter. Uncle Bob brought up his old top coat with a huge furry collar. It was snug, but a little ungainly. Aunt Bea was gracious enough to by me a leather jacket, bomber style, that lasted all through school and them some. It was particularly appreciated when I played outdoors hockey.

That's one thing I did enjoy about Nfld. was the hockey. We played in the streets or wherever we could find ice. Here at the seminary we played on the lake or flooded the football field. I remember helping to do this by hooking up a fire hose at night when the temperature was about 5 degrees above zero. Pretty neat the way the water practically froze when it hit the ground.

Winter time at the sem was joyous with a lot of outdoor stuff. We tobogganed down suicide hill which was an ice-filled chute onto the lake. We made fracture producing jumps down the ol'suicide for both toboggan and skiers who knew no fear or equipment.

Skis in the 50's where mostly strap on, cumbersome things, just waiting for an accident to happen. A lot of the fellows came to chapel and study hall with foam donuts to sit on.

Routine at the seminary was very controlled. The philosophy of obedience to the rule and the mind set of study when it's time to study; pray when it's time to pray and play when it's time to play.

Rule of the Day

5:30 AM – Rise, Morning Prayers and Meditation. Mass.
6:45-7:30- Breakfast.
8:00- 8:30- Free time
8:30- 10:00 – Classes
10:00- 10:15 – Break
10:15-11:45 – Classes
11:45- 12:30 – Mid-day prayers and Lunch.
12:30- 1:15 – Free time.
1:15- 3:15 – Classes.
3:15- 5:00- Free time, intramural sports.
5:00- 5:45 – Study hall.
5:45- 6:30 – Chapel, Rosary, Dinner.
6:30- 7:30 – Free time.
7:30- 8:45- Study hall and spiritual reading.
8:45- 9:15- Chapel, night prayers.
9:15 PM- retire, lights out.

The above was the daily schedule, except on Wednesday and Saturday afternoons, which were free time from after lunch until study hall at 5:00 PM. Sunday schedule was also different, with a morning High Mass and free afternoons until 5:00 PM.

The food was very substantial and nourishing since most of it came from seminary's farm and cooked by the Salvatorian Sisters. Jam at

breakfast was a treat, deserts at lunch and dinner was usually jello or whatever. Once in a while we went daffy-duck over home made apple pie. In season we were blessed with some great apple orchards. Nothing like a "snowball" apple taken chilled from underneath an apple tree. This particular apple was small and very white and juicy on the inside. It was a great treat at the 10:00 morning break.

I became interested in archery and progressed from a 15# wood bow (which I snapped) to a Bear composite reflex 51# bow from Grayling, Michigan. This was the day of the long bow and the modern pulley type bows were not even around. When you pulled a 51# bow, you drew that weight and held it until release. Arrows were generally 11/32 cedar shaft with true feathers. I was a mighty hunter, particularly after chipmunks. They were a tough target, but I managed to skewer and skin enough to fashion a pelt. My best piece of the pelt was a very elusive gopher. This sneaky-Pete had a hole on the side of the football bowl. He would journey a short distance from the entrance but would retreat at the least approach of a student, and even more so when he sensed the mighty bow hunter.

One day as I was finishing a target shoot with my best cedar arrows I crept to within 30 yards of Mr. gopher who had by now positioned himself in his hole, half-way looking out at me. I let fly an arrow from my magnificent Cub bow. As he heard the string snap, down he went...but not quickly enough. Sneaky-Pete was added to the pelt.

Classes were for the most part less than inspiring or useful, unless one wanted to become a priest and celebrate church services in Latin. *"Amo, Amas, Amat"* well, this certainly is Latin for I love, you love, he loves, but learning the full spectrum of Latin took

many years. It was a discipline and helpful for brain development as was the farm food helpful in giving me a cast iron stomach. My four years at SDS (Salvatorian Seminary) did give me a healthy taunt body, mainly because of the disciplined life, almost daily pulling a 50# bow and eating few sweets. I'm not sure about my healthy mind when it comes to sexuality.

No, there never was any homosexuality that I was aware of. But the natural development of a young boy's body and genitals were not considered to be any other than something one must control, that is, never have a nasty thought, look at forbidden pictures, and most of all, never jack off. Wet dreams when they occurred were rather mysterious and desirable. I found myself at night rubbing my penis on the mattress subconsciously, or partially awake, enjoying the sensation, but aware of not "going too far." Although sometimes, squirts happened, much to my delight, but of course, I wasn't responsible because I was only half awake. I would confess these occurrences with the rationalization that I was half-asleep and therefore didn't sin; I wasn't impure. The priest hearing my confession usually agreed.

So I went through from 13 to 22 years, having hands off my dick, but getting away with mattress rubbing to find relief. I graduated from SDS and went to New York to continued my studies for the priesthood.

Summer Days While On Vacation

I had a couple of months before resuming my studies at a new seminary located in New York. This was a Junior Seminary and furnished the first two years of college, granting an Associate of Arts degree in Liberal Arts. It was a continuation of Latin, Greek, Italian languages, as well as some Science and Literature.

Before going to *Mater Christi* (as the seminary was called), I took on my first real job in the world as a clerk in a dry goods store. I secured the hefty wage of 78 cents an hour for a forty-eight hour week…ugg and double ugg. The work was absolutely boring. When I wasn't waiting on a customer, I had to look busy by straightening stock and stuff.

It did have some good features like the young girl who measured 19" around the waist I measured for a pair of Levis. There were others, who measured more. One in particular, an Italian girl who when she came out of the dressing room, her mother remarked: "Take off those jeans, they look like a skin on a baloney."

Next door was a drug store soda fountain where I would go on break. There was a really cute girl there named Elaine. She would fix me coffee and an English muffin. She wore a white short skirt uniform and I had a really hard time trying not to bone-up. She enhanced my half-awake mattress rubbings.

Also there was Cathy from my Third Grade infatuation. She worked at a park as a counselor and wore tight yellow short shorts. I chatted with her, but she was somewhat aloof when she learned I was going to be a priest. I had dreamed of riding my Triumph motorcycle to her house and taking her for a ride to some secluded spot and screwing her brains out.

Actually, I didn't have a Triumph. I had a Vespa scooter. My brother Ralph came home one day with a 500 cc BSA bike. I lusted after this beauty. I was given a chance to ride it as he watched. I gave it the same amount of gas I gave to my Vespa, and the difference being 0 to 60 mph in four seconds as I blasted by my watching and horrified brother. The Vespa wide opened only went 36 mph in 36 seconds with its pitiful 150 cc engine.

My brother's friend had a Triumph Thunderbird for sale. It was a 650 cc beauty which I would have died for. Dad and I went to try it out and I flew like the wind. The price was $400 and Dad was just about to buy it for me when the greedy owner said "Oh, I need $40 more for the saddle bags." Dad said he'd have to think about it. When Mom was consulted she expressed concern and said she rather I didn't get a bike just now. Oh, the pain and disappointment that followed.. I dreamed of that nacelle (headlamp and odometer) with the tach and speedo climbing to 60-70-80 mph. I dreamed of Cathy on the back with her yellow short-shorts and me checking for my billfold. Oopsie, impure thought!

Mater Christi, the New Seminary

Well, here we are, 17 years old and going to my first year of college. I couldn't believe how great this place was. I had an actual room, with one roommate, not a dormitory. There was a closet, not a locker, and a private sink and mirror. Still had the communal showers and john. I previously had a john problem in Wisconsin, due to the urinals close proximately to each other. Kids would stand right next to you while taking a leak, and sometimes there would be one kid wait to use yours. Well, for some reason, I had a hard time peeing under this condition and would have to try to go when the john was empty or there were very few kids using it. What a pain.

This occurred the first time when I was traveling and was at a train station using a like type urinal in a crowded john with people waiting to pee. I was locked up. The guy behind me said, "Hey kid, you gonna pee or what?" That did it. I couldn't and have had this problem every since.

The fellow students were all just out of regular High School, mostly Catholic High Schools. I was amazed at the impurity at these schools. One guy we called the Moth would recount how a lunch times he would get this girl and have "coffee." This was an euphemism slipping it to her under her shot pleated school uniform skirt while she dropped her panties. Coffee was served standing up in the locker room.

Another story shocked me about the "Ghost." Seems the Catholic school when playing another school in basketball had a secret weapon called the Ghost. If the opposing team had a high scorer, they would send in the ghost who would disable the high scorer with a kick in the balls.

All in all though I really enjoyed the camaraderie, the studies and some of the profs. Well, one in particular didn't like me. He was the Chemistry prof and one day we were to heat Early Meyer flasks on Bunsen burners. I tried to heat mine but didn't remove the asbestos plate between the burner and the flask. Oopsie, the prof noticed, became unglued and called me a Nincompoop. Poor fellow, he use to smoke 3 packs of Camels a day, probably not around any longer. Speaking of ciggies, wow, Marlboros 18 cents a pack. We all smoked like furnaces, except, we could only smoke outside during breaks. Do you know how good a ciggie tastes when you are limited to certain time? Anyway, I was mostly a pipe smoker. I remember Hart, as he sucked the guts out of a Lucky and exclaimed: "Heaven would be a never ending Lucky Strike." There was also "Fats" who would take an unfiltered Chesterfield and take three deep drags in succession with no noticeable exhale. Probably came out of his ass.

In Between, Before the Rock

Our summers were spent as Camp Counselors at Camp Tekakwitha on lovely Lake Luzerne, just below Lake George, NY. Fun with boys 8 through early teens. Lot of swimming, sports and just all around fun. The day started with early morning Mass and prayers. The chapel was down a wooden path and rustically beautiful.

I taught archery and had a little fat boy who could barely draw the fiber glass bow. As his arrow never really reached the hay bale target, I would always say "Nice try, Sid, almost." He replied: "Well, if I'm so good, how come I can't hit the target." He never found out. He wasn't all that well like as some kid peed in his canteen.

The Rock

Having graduated with my AA degree, I was sent to St. Bernard Seminary in Rochester, New York. We call it the Rock, because it is a most foreboding castle like stone edifice, complete with iron gates, fences and some bars...not the kind at Lake George.

We continued to wear cassocks, a clerical garb that's like a dress with a lot of buttons, topped off with a white Roman collar around the neck. The routine was almost as rigid as my early sem days at SDS. There were hardly any smiles and not much fun. Classes were in Latin and mostly meaningless if you were to equate them with reality. Not much fun other than play handball and bridge, smoking and looking forward to scant vacations. The Rock broke me after I received my BA in Philosophy and continued to a semester of post-grad work in Theology I came home and told Mom, it is not for me.

I was home from the seminary, home for good. It was around Christmas time, and I had made the decision in 1960, at the age of 22 to begin a new life. Nobody was home at my parents' house and I felt like a drink. My first real drink. I called the liquor store and asked if they delivered, not having any wheels at the time. I also asked what might be a good whiskey that was affordable. The guy on the other end of the line was a nice guy, patient and helpful. He said that "Ten High" by Hiram Walker was a good four year old bourbon, sour mash and $3.95 delivered. A done

deal! I poured one shot glass ½ full and savored the dark brown, deliciously scented booze. It warmed me immediately and I felt a little nervous, as I didn't want to be sick. You see, at the age of 19, I went to a seminarian party here in Schenectady, where the partygoers were all regular high school graduates, just newly entered into the seminary. They could hold their beer. For me it was new experience, and I got totaled on 2 beers. Boy, was I sick. I had to sleep over. The boys tried to help me walk it off, but to no avail. They called my folks to tell them that I was zonked out and would be home in the morning. I didn't want to get sick again.

Home for the Holidays, and then Some

Mom and Dad were great, no problem having Mr. Mo home. Dad suggested since I would become A1 candidate for the draft, and he didn't mean having another Bud, I'd best decide what to do about the military.

I signed up with the Air Force Officer Candidate program and took a series of tests in Rome NY. While there I went to the "O" club for a drink and to check out the girls.

I was practicing some dance steps out of a book at home and wanted to try them out on a live girl. I asked this rather cute one, who was sitting, if she would like to dance. She said sure and stood up, all 4'5". She came up to my belt buckle. Looking at the top of her head was going to be a position I would enjoy in time to come, but right at this moment, my virginal/celibate instinct and training thought nothing but let's dance. I stumbled through it, bought her a drink and retired to the Officers Bachelor Quarters.

Back home it was time to get a job, my first one. I applied as a data entry clerk at the Bureau of Tax and Finance, state of NY. I took the typing test and past at a phenomenal speed of 28 wpm.

The Bureau was a building of some 500 sex starved women and 3 men. The other two men told me they were sex starved. I was interested because my only female acquaintance since returning from the sem was a sixteen year old named Nancy. I took Nancy

skating and when she fell down I reached under her arms and got a feel of young breast. Wow! After hot chocolate I took her home; her father was waiting

Next, Nancy and I went bowling. Seems that bowling is going to play some importance in my life other than playing with my ol' Navy buddies for Ballentine Ale and 10cents a strike and 5cents a spare. Anyway, we had strict instructions to be home before midnight. We smooched, very tenderly and chastely until about 12:45. Dad was a bit irritated to the point that he thought I might be too old for Nancy and don't come back. I don't know if Nancy ever recovered. I saw her years later and she was a mother of three.

My social life took a turn for the better, actually, I wasn't on any road at all. A very effervescent, rather rotund chap headed the local CYO- the Catholic Young Adult League. It was made up of folks much like the moth and coffee drinkers, remember the moth and his coffee at high school? They were planning a Dude Ranch weekenderbender which was going to be near Lake George, of happy memory. Back in the days when I was a seminarian camp counselor, my fellow Camp Counselor, Bob, and I motored over on the Vespa to check out such a ranch. We saw some guys ambling down the path followed by some pretty randy looking chicks. The guys definitely looked like they were exhausted. Actually, they looked like they had just screwed their brains out and were now on automatic.

Before this happening however, I attended a cocktail party and watched as a petite Italian beauty in a crinoline skirt, of all things, mounted the top of a piano, while her dad played <u>Dixie Melody.</u> Maryann belted it out in grand style and I took a liking to the singing and a peek up skirt.

Later, at work, luck would have it that Maryann worked as a keypunch operator at the same place. We wrote each other little notes on the IBM cards and got together for lunch. She mounted my Vespa side saddle and off we went into the country. She surely was young and pretty. After small talk and a sandwich, I leaned over and kissed her. Wow. She said she wasn't that kind of girl, and don't try anything funny. I think she like it though.

My performance as a keypunch operator really sucked. My supervisor, Rose, a nice married Italian with pronounced bosom, covered for me. I like to hang around Maryann and her redhead girlfriend, Carol. Carol had a steady and was going at it steady. She shared her experiences with Maryann and wondered when Mr. Mo was going to go down on her.

Not too long afterwards, Maryann and the entire CYO groupies and groupies headed to the Dude Ranch outing. I knew something good was going to happen, as Maryann taught me how to really kiss. We were in my Dad's 1960 Ford, parked near her house on a date return, when she reached over and planted a big one on me, long and hard, tonsil sucking kiss. My brain when numb as all my blood rushed to my dick. Giggling, she went up the porch.

At the ranch I bought along a fifth of Ballentine Scotch which we savored chasing it down with, would you believe, Schaffer beer. We danced the night away, square dancing of all things. A break now and them to snort scotch and lay under a tree kissing and making eyes at each other. Gee, romance is so very good. Other CYOers began bedding each other etc. I wasn't there yet.

The next day found Maryann and I laying on her bed, kissing. Kissing long and hard, not even coming up for air. I had a bonner,

but that was not my concern. I had my hand down here jean front, under the elastic of her panties. I put a finger in her snatch. If felt really good. Then, after some time, another finger, and then three. It was just wonderful. I didn't even think of screwing or asking for a blow job. I wasn't there yet, I was still a virgin.

The Navy

Well, the Air Farce said I was quoted out and to reapply sometime later. Yeah, right. Down to the friendly Navy recruiter, if you have a college degree and are breathing, the Navy signs you up for Officer Candidate School.

I told Maryann I have to go to Newport RI, and she said I should do the best I can, she would write and remain faithful.

So, off I go to become an Ensign in the US Navy Reserve. Boy, it was tough, march, drill, study, sweat exams everyday etc. Once they got you, if you wash out, into the fleet as a Seaman Apprentice for two years. Clever program.

I studied hard and was making it. Maryann wrote daily, scorching love letters, humerous cards and just a great girl friend.

I visited some chums in Newport, one of my ol' Bernard guys was there. He had a sister who was OK. She asked me what kind of ship I would like to be on when I graduated. I said, "Oh, maybe a carrier or amphibious vessel." She asked: "How about a LMC?" What the heck is an LMC? Sounds like an amphib ship, like LST, LSD etc. I said, "Yeah, that would be nifty." She asked me if I knew what a LMC was. I said, well, what. "Large Mahogany Chair." We all laughed at my expense.

I was really getting the hots for Maryann. We made a clandestine date to meet in New York City. She would drive down with her girl friend Margaret and we would spend a day and night together. What a fine time, we toured, had a spaghetti dinner at an outside café and then to the hotel room. Margaret pretended to sleep while Maryann and I joined our underwear clad bodies and kissed fervently. The closest we came to sex so far us when Maryann dry-humped me in my parents bed. We both came. I felt really guilty. So I lowered my Navy issued boxer shorts and tried to penetrate. Her vagina was too small. I'm not bragging, but it was too small. I pushed and pushed, but hard as I was, I couldn't get it in.

I withdrew with a popping sound, and thought this was OK. God bless. And we fell asleep. I returned to base the next day, not entirely fulfilled, but not unfulfilled either. I really loved that girl.

Before long I purchased a one quarter carat diamond, an Artcraft, for $175. It really broke me as I was only earning $78 a month. But it was a nice ring. I called Maryann and asked her to marry me over a 3 minute phone call and that I was bringing a ring home next weekend.

Graduation was wonderful since I passed and became an Ensign in the US Navy Reserve. My folks and Maryann and her folks all journeyed to Newport for the event. I thought I looked dashing in my Officer's uniform, with the single gold brad on the sleeve crowned with a star. I really like the officer's cap, with its striking shield of eagle, cross anchors and flag emblem.

I started to adopt an air of arrogance as I preened and strutted about. I had a few days leave before reporting to my ship at Norfolk VA.We were planning a February wedding and then disaster struck

several times. First, Maryann's mother, Gladys, didn't particularly like me or my parents. She wanted to invite most of Italy to the wedding and wanted my parents to help with the bill. Mom said her obligation was to give the rehearsal dinner and boutonnières for the ushers. She told Gladys that she read this in a book on Weddings. "A book!, She read it in a book!" Gladys exclaimed. Things started to go down a very steep hill. My ushers, a randy, rowdy bunch were invited to a meeting at Gladys house. I asked her to server beer and pretzels; she came up with pie and coffee. Having left her pie and coffee untouched we proceeded to the bar to discuss preparations. She was off the wall.

The final debacle, small as it was, took place at the bowling alley. I went with Tom, an ol' friend from keypunch days and his current lay. Tom liked to pump iron and invite younguns to his apartment where he donned spandex briefs and strut around with the weights. The girls were hopeless, lot of gutter balls, tee, hee. Tom and I decided to bowl a game without the tee, hees and asked them to smoke and drink while we did manly bowling. Maryann wanted to bowl with us and I declined. That was it! Can you imagine. My ring was returned to my Mom the next day and I was unable to contact her before I left for my shipboard assignment in Norfolk.

I'm in the Navy Now

Norfolk, Virginia is commonly pronounced Norfuck by the Fleet. This hold true for most of the officers of the US Navy, but for the enlisted, they get laid almost anytime they want.

I was endeavoring to break the celibate life style of my fellow officers on board the USS Nonuki. I ran into a local who I was fortunate to party with and this led to an introduction to the Portsmouth Nursing School of bedable , earthy, smart nurses. I snaked my friend's girlfriend while he was out of town and asked her if she and some of her friends would like to come aboard for a great movie and drinks and dancing at the O club afterward.

I arrived with main date and three luscious babes and ferried them into the ward room.Uggh, my colleagues were strewn about in lackadaisical fashion displaying nothing working for them whatsoever. The girls picked up on this, but stayed anyway. No one got up, no one greeted them or showed the least amount of interest. One of the girls asked if they were all gay. I tried to encourage a little response other than farting and snoring from the kaki clad oafs. I took the girls to the O club and upon entrance, they were snatched up by, of all things, Marine aviators.

Marines are an unusual bunch. Once, when a young lady got on a crowded bus, two marines were sitting together and one of them got up and said: "Here Ma'am, have my f-cin' seat." As the lady sat down a bit miffed, the other marine said: "You'll have to excuse

my buddy Ma'am, he's not too suave when it comes to talking to you cunts."

Another incident took place in the basement of the Portsmouth O club where some of my wimpy fellow officers with nothing working for us were knocking down a pitcher of suds when the table of marines sitting adjacent to us began sing derogatory songs. We responded with like melodies and they responded with tossing several glasses of brew our way to which we responded with a whole pitcher. Oopsie, chairs went flying and I also was catapulted across the room and slid into the juke box. Well, sensing destruction, mainly our own, I challenged the largest of the marines to a fight: "Choose your weapon, Dude." He reached into his pocket and said: "Knives, Mother..." No greater love can a fellow officer give to his shipmates then to lay down his life for their safety. Not this one. I scrammed out the door with 2nd Lieutenant Franksteing following with his blade. Facilely, I leaped into my VW and shouted as I turned on the lights and headed straight for my adversary: "I choose Volkswagens." Narrowly missing him, I headed back for the safety of the ship.

Would you believe I am still a virgin? We deployed to the Caribbean, and hit a liberty port at Santa Domingo. I was casually talking to a pretty native and she suggested we go upstairs to get better acquainted. Bingo, this may be it.

We ascended to a small desk behind which a guy offers me a towel and wants five dollars for the room. I had a five and a couple of singles. We entered the room and she turned down the light and began blowing me. Felt really good, and she then inserted me into a hot, wet cunt. My first real penetration, but alas, as I was repositioning myself, not having cum, she slipped me out and

37

slipped into the bathroom. This was not a really great first-timer. She came back and wanted money; all I had was two dollars, half a pack of Luckies and a pocket knife. She said that was OK.

I got back to the ship and told my Bunkie, Jack, my fears of getting the clap as I did not use a rubber. He laughed and said: "Don't worry, it will probably just shrivel up and fall off." Thanks Jack. Jack was a vivacious enjoyable guy, who always seemed to get propositioned by queers. He would lay in the top bunk reading "NewYorker" and comment on poetry. I think he was bi-sexual in that he would regale me with stories of Hillary, a raven haired white skinned beauty whom he enjoyed dicking at long length. He would describe how he could insert and remain hard for hours. Dunno how he could do that.

Years later I went to see Jack and his debutant wife in Manhattan. Linda said we were going to a party of gays that night and please don't be offended. We went and Jack disappeared with some guys just as soon as we arrived. I rather enjoyed the party and no one hit on me.

I lost track of Jack, I think he went to SanFran and last I heard, died there. I suspect AIDS got him.

Having lost my virginity, I was now prepared for further losses. The next dalliance was Jamaica. We went to an officers' party ashore and Graham a fellow Ensign, and I left really stoned. We were walking down the street next to a vacant lot when we heard a "Pst." Out of the woods comes a native propositioning us for a screw or blow job behind a bush. Five dollars would do it. We asked if she had a bed somewhere and she said she did, but her brother was sleeping

in it and if we would come back here in an hour, she would make herself and the bed available. Her name was Rosey.

We continued on and ended up in a bar with two native prostitutes. Graham followed one upstairs and tried to get a freebie. Bad choice as he was chased half naked across the roof by her guardian. I paid my the five she asked for and this time slipped on a rubber. She asked if I came more than once, please put on a new rubber, as she said sometimes the used one slips off into her cunt and its hard to get out. They say "Once Black, never back." Which saying has the credibility of "I won't come in your mouth."

I never again paid five dollars for a piece of ass, nevertheless, I never slept alone until I was married.

Getting laid in Norfuck (Norfolk VA) was not going to happen. I was somewhat dating a sexy divorcee who stopped at kissyface. When I deployed, she asked if she could take care of my 1960 VW. Sure, why not? Later, I got a shipboard phone call from Darlene, her sister-in-law, who said I should give her the power of attorney to reclaim my auto before Suzy completely destroys it.

When I returned to base and got my auto back, it was a mess. A sticky substance was all over the place, sailors' clothes and baby diapers and stuff added to the interior which was not longer leak proof due to a slashed convertible top. Gads Suzy, what did you do?

I tracked her down as a waitress in a bar on Main Street. She looked affright, and puffy, lumpy and maybe preggers. Didn't have much to say .

I learned of a hungry girl in Washington DC where a friend of mine assured me she would be an easy lay. I journey to her pad, and off we went to a secluded beach after having stopped at a drug store to "pick up some blades." This was the code word for getting some rubbers. Laying on a towel I became amorous and slipped off her one piece bathing suit. Ever try removing one of these? Whew. She was soft and white and young. I slipped on a rubber on my roaring hardon and went to town. It was a little gritty due to the sand, but got off OK. We returned to her mother's house and they put me up for the night. My quicky really didn't satisfy me and I thought of sneaking into her room. I chickened out.

The next day she invited me to her father's apartment in DC. I remember her wearing traditional, rather baggy, yellow panties. I don't even remember her name, what she looked like or even kissing her. I just took off the undies and dropped my load. Really a slam, bam and not even thank you M'am, What a cad I am. She was looking for a bit of tenderness and wondered if she would every see me again. I just replied "Gotta race." I left.

So far, sexual experiences have been infantile, except for the passionate embraces of Maryann that happened shortly after leaving the Seminary..

Europe and the Med

Now that my virginity was in the past tense, my life of celibacy in Norfuck had to change. I requested duty in Washington DC (Desiring Cunt). Washington was a mecca of available women, the ration was about 8 girls to 1 guy. Oh, happy government girl-employment days.

My XO (Executive Officer) said he knew a Detailer (Navy placement officer) and perhaps he could find me a billet in DC. Sure enough, I was offered a cushy job in the Naval Observatory as Head of Translations Section, ONI (Office of Naval Intelligence). You see, I had a lot of language qualifications, important ones, like Latin, Greek, Hebrew and assorted romance languages. The Detailer thought I would be committing career suicide by leaving shipboard duties after only one and a half years of sea duty. Oh man, suicide here I come.

We were just getting ready to depart for a Med (Mediterranean) cruise and I asked the skipper to detach me with my new orders to DC. He said why not come on the cruise and he would detach me in Naples so I could travel Europe before flying back to the states. I said I couldn't afford it and he replied he go into hock for a year to take such a trip. Accordingly, I asked Mom and Dad for a $300 loan. I paid it back, most kids don't, I know mine never did.

Off to Naples. On route I was OD (Officer of the Deck) while steaming in formation. I was ill equipped for navigational duties

and on top of that I was a nerd. As the ship slipped out of station, that is we were falling behind the other ships because I decreased ever so slightly the RPM of the screws by mistake. The captain came roaring out on the bridge and asked who has the Conn. He was a lion of a man, full of fury. I stuttered and said some asinine thing: "Ahh, Captain, I just came out of CIC." What a nerd I was, skinny, wearing ridiculous heavy black rimmed glasses, smacking my lips. He looked at me like he was regarding a dog who had just dumped on the living room carpet.

Well, even so, I was promoted to LTJG and had a wetting down party at Rota Spain. Getting smashed as usual, I decided to join the floor show where the girls where doing a hot Flamingo dance routine. My debut was quickly terminated by two bulky ushers who picked me up and carried my back to my seat.

My buddy, Sinclair, another fellow officer getting detached for a new duty station, and I arrived at Naples and left our mother ship. Absolutely no hard feelings. We rented a VW and proceeded to the Allied Officers Club to load the entire back seat with booze. We placed a huge bottle of Chianti between and motored toward Rome in search of skirts.

The Chianti lasted half way there so we stopped for a refill along with hard crusty bread, cheese and salami. The shop took our empty and replaced it with a like size bottle with no top. You see, they pour a little mineral oil, or something like that on top of the refilled bottle instead of a stopper. I took a lusty swig and spat out the oil. All the Italians laughed at such a nerd. I never did learn how they get at the wine and not drink the oil.

At the leaning tower of Pisa we encountered our first girls. Nothing to look at really, but we tried to invoke a little interest. We asked them if they got hit on because they were two girls traveling alone. They said sure and that they have a code. If the situation looked unpromising, they would sing "Moon River" which was the code to bail as soon as possible. Also they carried a wicked looking knife if the situation deteriorated.

Speaking of knives, I stopped at a little Italian knife shop and purchased a genuine prohibition era pearl handled switch blade. I mean, the real thing. Long lean and sharp. The proprietor put a keen blade on it and it is still razor sharp today, after almost 40 years. The mechanism is superb, and the blade springs out with great authority. It is just made for sticking into someone. I love it. I almost lost it on one of my odysseys. I was traveling down the east coast of Michigan on a motorcycle adventure and stopped to have my old horsehide motorcycle jacket repaired. This is one of the last all time great authentic bad-ass leather jackets made of horse hide, not cow hide or other finky stuff. I had my stiletto in the upper zip pocket for emergency defensive use and it apparently fell out while the authentic mc jacket was being healed. I noticed my blade missing when I returned home and called the shoe repair shop. I remembered the guy's name and he remembered me and said he had the knife and would I like it back? What a gem. He mailed it the next day. I noticed he was using it to cut leather as there was some residue, but you know what, the blade was still as sharp as ever.

We arrived in Rome, still seeking to get laid. The opportunity seem to present itself in the form of a night club entertainer. She said if

we waited til after her 2 AM performance, we might get together. Well, we struggled through a lot of drinks and tried to stay awake. When we woke up at the table as we had crashed, Donna was gone and forgotten. We probably couldn't get one up anyway.

Before France, we decided on a trip to Switzerland. We crossed over the border of Italy and attempted to enter Switzerland. No dice. The guard said our orders did not include them. We couldn't get back into Italy either, there was something wrong. Finally, a dapper European gent told us the Italian gate guard was looking for our insurance papers before admitting us. Fortunately, the papers were in the glove box and we were on our way to Paris.

Rambling down the Champ Elysee, Sinclair and I sat down at a cozy sidewalk café and introduced ourselves to two girls sipping warm beer. Nan and Zelda were from Germany living in France as nannies. They hadn't been on a date for a year due to the crudeness of the French boys. We assured them that we were gentlemen and asked them to join us for the Follies Berge and dinner. This was the start of a three day date, which was utopia.

When I returned to the States, Zelda began writing me, her letters included crushed flowers, she wanted to come live with me. A case of GU...geographically undesirable. Oh well, vive la France and the German connection, unfortunately unconnected.

Back to the Good Ol' USA and D.C.

First of all a pad, a place to live. After checking out some efficiencies that would be slumming it, unattractive, a few roaches, small, dark, lonely and just not me. The criterion was affordability and at $84 a month, these offerings of efficiency apartments met the criterion. I saw an ad for a roommate in Arlington VA. I called and went for an interview with the other roommates: Bruce, the owner and a social worker; Bill, Navy engineer; Ron, oceanographer; Tom a chemist; Spence a seismologist and then came Mo, a LTJG, USNR.

The interview went OK and I was accepted into the household. Pretty good deal, $50 a month included house keeper who would shovel the place out once a week. We had three refrigerators and cooked our own stuff. Kitchen duties rotated. Not bad at all. We called the house the "Pershing House" as it was located on Pershing Avenue.

My first week there we had a weekender bender open house party. We gave cards out to any good looking girl in D.C. inviting them to the bash and telling them to bring a friend if they so desired. We fixed up the back yard with three full kegs and assorted muchies here and there. With coordinated vests to indicate we were the hosts, we welcomed tons of female flesh and so noted their arrival in a Guest Book, complete with phone numbers.

One girl in particular caught my fancy on the couch. A slim brunette in a short tennis skirt passed out with legs apart revealing

white panties matching her short tennis skirt. After a close look and smell, I slid the panties down to her knees and admired smooth young fragrant veldt and a closed slit hiding the inner lips of wet and warmth. Still the good Catholic boy, I pulled up her panties and left her to snooze unmolested, or rather just a little molested.

The next day the roomies got together and annotated the list of girls in the Guest Book as to desirability. We had groovy contacts to call for dates for the next month or so. Clever guys we were.

There was one in particular that I had met previously at a Navy office party. Her name was Pamela and she was opening beers with a church key and I was able to get a phone number. I called Pamela after the Pershing House beer blast. She didn't care much for the party as the competition was fierce, and I didn't pay much attention to her. We made a date which she tried to cancel, the bitch! She worked in the Pentagon and asked who was the new LTJG in OpM4? She didn't even remember my name, the bitch! The head of OpM4, a Navy Captain, asked Pamela why she wanted to know? She said she made a date with the guy and wanted to cancel, the bitch! The Captain said: "We don't break dates with fellow officers."

I picked up Pam with my snappy VW convertible, a blue bug newly constituted after Suzy screwed her brains out with Navy enlisted in Norfolk. Oh, remember my mention of a brief try at a beautiful raven haired gal I briefly encountered in Norfolk?. When I deployed (went to sea) I left her my VW. She trashed it.

Pam and I went to the Potomac River for a concert. We rented a canoe and paddled to the Carton Barron theatre, and tied up near the stage. Pretty romantic except for the turds that floated down

the river, ugg, raw sewage. Dunno what the situation today is, but back in the 60's pretty rank.

Well, Pam and I got along just right. One night after a full shaker of Manhattans made with Hiram Walker Ten High, I lifted her skirt on the couch, slid down the panties and plunged in to incredible warm, wet great smelling female heaven. I drove home that night so satisfied and kept smelling my fingers, exotic fragrance Being the good Catholic boy, I dated Pam and she was the only one I had sex with. She wondered what my intentions were and I said "Marriage?" It really didn't occur to me until she brought up the subject. So I proposed and she said "yes."

That's when the sex ended. She wanted to save herself until marriage that was six months in the future. Funny thing about Pam. We married and I never slept alone until then. Well, perhaps an exaggeration, but she surely was frosty until she decided she wanted children, and then it was every day until preggers.

Westward Ho

The Navy stint ended and Pam and I decided to follow Lewis and Clark in a VW Camper. The adventure began in NY and ended in California. Met some interesting folks along the way. One in particular were Tim and Cathy. They had a VW camper like ours only a little more ragged and sporting flower stickers. Yeah, flower children complete with little girl and cat. The cat got eaten by a badger in Canada where we first met these guys. We saw them again in the middle of Detroit and arranged to meet at Glacier National Park.

Glacier Park was a hike to the glacier some eight mile up. We trudged along hauling the kid and some pine cones Pam strapped on my back with some dynamite wire she found. Although the idea of a bang was appealing I doubt I had the energy. We arrived at the summit toward evening and went to the lodge for accommodations...sorry, no room at the Inn. This is were the little girl came in handy as we said there was no way we could make the return trip in the dark, especially since the Forest Ranger told us of a recently half-eaten horse by a bear that was discovered on the path. So, the Park Rangers gave us their cabin, how nice. Pam and I slept in a double, and I was awaken by Pam needing to take a leak. Since there was only the outhouse down the path, I suggested she go there as I told her it was perfectly safe and that "there was nothing out there." She replied: "There can be anything out there. Get up and go with me." I did. As we were walking to the outhouse,

she decided just to squirt on the path. Suddenly, there arose such a clatter...a huge white object came leaping across the porch of the cabin and started a full advance upon us. It was a giant ram, not an SUV, but close to one in size. I did the manly thing and distracted the beast by pounding some rocks together, making menacing noises. Pam hiked up her panties and fled. I followed and arrived on the porch and observed the beast looking up at me. I needed to wiz also, so I unzipped and let off a stream of hot piss. The beast started to lap it up, and, to my dismay, began to eye my Johnson as if to do some gobbling. Well, I'm not into that, especially if none one informed Mr. Whitely that teeth are not allowed in such an action. I zipped and quit.

The next great adventure occurred in San Francisco. Pam decided it was time to seek work and live a while in SanFran. One of my interviews was with a fire alarm company during which I was informed that everyone has a major fire in their lives. That evening I was cooking something on the stove, clad in my shorts. I moved to close to the flame and pooof, my first major fire...hot pants.

Took a job selling infant formula. I developed a saying:" Doctor, it's Similac, or bust, or both." That little ditty sold a lot to cans of Similac. Of course, the secret to seeing the doctors was to catch them in their hospital rounds or find a way to ingratiate oneself with the nurses at the office. No problem. I always had a bag full of goodies and they liked me because I was fast and jovial with their boss.

Had a California kid. After the first born son, sex became non existent, although the need to unload fostered by my reptilian brain, sought Merry Hand and her four sisters. The problem was trying to stay awake while switching hands.

Porn to the rescue. One hot day, a week day, I had to find relief for my Johnson which was twitching in my jeans. I had a copy of Playboy which featured a hot Asian girl in a mini. I went to the back room of the porch and proceeded to jerk off. Oopsie, along comes Pam. I think I avoided the shameful detection, but I'm not quite sure. There is always the possibility of a spouse coming in at just the wrong time. Although this has not happened to me, there have been some close calls. I don't know what I would do if "Lovey" caught me with my jeans around my ankles spanking the monkey in front of internet newsgroup porn. Geeesssh. It's like the old joke of the guy in an airplane (the days of propeller craft and free smokes on the plane) who is sitting next to lady. He take out Playboy, turns to the centerfold and wacks his ham. He folds the mag, turns to the lady and says: "Pardon me M'am, mind if I smoke?"

Where is all this going?

I conquered the California turf I was assigned and was looking for management. I had a meeting with the VP in SanFran and over copious martinis; I accepted a job as an Academician Rep in Boston. Calling on the major teaching hospitals and trying to influence Pediatric residents to use Similac etc. I met with some resistance. Seems the department heads were repulsed by "sales" types. I did OK thought with throwing beer parties at the residents dormitories and was appreciated for the largess of free Similac for those who had small ones. I still got postage paid reply cards asking for Similac five years after I moved on to another job.

The Other Job: Computers

I made a major bad move and mistake. I could have stayed with pharmaceuticals and enjoyed eventual management and early retirement with great perks, but the allure of selling main frame computer systems with high commissions and large base salary was just too tempting. I snagged a job with a major manufacturer by writing a follow-up thank you note referring to O'Diorne's <u>Management by Objectives</u> which was my prospective boss's hot button.

After six months of computer training classes, which were somewhat enhanced by Elise. You see, Elise was 19 and wore a very short mini-skirt. She had a radiant complexion, long athletic legs, glorious blond hair and I think nice boobs, although my eyes seldom rose above the exposed thigh and hint of panties.

Won some, loss some, the computer game was a toughie. Back in the 70's there was Snow White (IBM) and the seven dwarfs: Xerox, RCA, NCR, Burroughs, Honeywell, CDC and Univac. There were large marketing budgets and rewards. A small system of a 16KB (memory) mainframe, with card-reader, and tape storage, and COBOL, would sell for a quarter million dollars and lease for about $4800 a month. Add a 30MB disk and you would increase the cost by $1400. Commissions were 3% of the purchase price.

One of my fellow sales reps was Jack, a cool guy. He closed a biggie and bought himself a Eldorado with *Nine Liter* written on the

side. He was hanging with Elise who he escorted to Florida for some true love and dope. Got caught and spent some time in the slammer.

Breakout

Hey, time to scoot. I sold a biggie, made a sales training video and was offered a really cushy job as a sales trainer. What a fine time, introducing new hire sales to the technology and sales tactics for computer marketing.

It was especially fun since these were the days of "Affirmative Action."

Like, we hire ladies! The sales classes were three weeks in duration. One guy remarked: "Some of us have been here for a while. Even the crack of dawn was looking good."

One guy in particular was a real "get some-guy." He was a southern who just had to get nightly laid. Not that good looking, but pretty smooth and had something the ladies just went down for.

Of course we had the ladies. Gail came in with shades one morning. What happened? She was in the old Boston Combat Zone, drinking. The bar keep took her glass, and she hadn't finished her drink. She said "Hey Fucker, bring that glass back!" Instead he gave her two shots to the face and blackened her eyes.

Back to Sales

After telling folks how to do it, it was time to get back into the field. Need some current sales to qualify for the cushy job of Sales Manager. I located south of the Gnat line and courted a really big manufacturer to replace an antiquated Burroughs system. I had all the right moves, right price and solutions. Right there dude! The wimpy good ol' boy controller was tracking just right, especially after I brought him cigars and visited him in the hospital after his hemorrhoid operation. He told me that corporate was sending down the Data Processing Manager to put in a spare System 3/15 (IBM) they had. Geeessh. I told him it would not work with the process control set up I had designed for him and that not only would it not work, it was absolutely not cost effective, etc, etc. The wimp said his hands were tied. So, I jumped the chain of command, went to Corporate in Chicago and had my head handed to me.

Things were looking bleak as my company was counting on the sale. My immediate boss was a blow hard and a heavy DeWar's Scotch drinker who had absolutely nothing working for him. He had a sidekick who was as fruity as they come who was making smart remarks about how I queered the deal. He should know, hey? Anyway, time to bail.

Landed a little further south and into Hot Atlanta. What a great city while

Underground was still the going thingy. All set with a great company when the little fart of a sales manager decided to pass on me and hire someone to work Florida. So, I took a fall-back job and crashed. What an outfit. I was telling the Sales Manager that we had a problem with our base accounts, because of continual hardware problems with a poorly designed disk drive. He said: "Don't bother about it, just FFFF!" I asked what did that mean"

Feel 'em, Find 'em, Fuck 'em and Forget 'em." Nice philosophy. I quite that day.

Life was not good. I had Pam up north trying to sell a really stupid big house and I was without a job. I took a little solace in a visit to the local porn store. Creeped into a booth laden with cum shots all over the wall and a odor to match. Slipped my quarters into the peek show and wacked my Johnson in my pants. Splat, all done. Not very satisfying and messy.

The trip back and forth to North Carolina was exhausting. You know, I never had a happy experience in NC other than a stint as an adjunct professor at a local Catholic college. I taught in the Adult Degree Division a course entitled "Introduction to Theology." All adult students needed this credit to graduate, so I had not disciplinary problems. I focused on Spirituality and always asked the question on exams: True or False: All holiness is relational? Most got it right.

North Carolina is where I first experienced bi-sexual tendencies. While moteling it, I picked up some porn, among which was a mag featuring youngsters in white BVDs. I found my Johnson quickening at the sight and imagined some oral and anal possibilities. This bi-sensuality grew to awesome dimensions with eventual separation

and divorce. Sexuality was a big part of my divorce, as my Pam was frigid to glacier proportions. Matter of fact in my diary keeping I drew a black line on the side of the pages indicating no sex and the line extended down the side of the diary covering over ¾ of the year! Ouch, extreme lacka (lack-of-sex).

Perhaps it's time to offer some writings that I did to express my depth of sexual desires and the influence of pornography that so captivated me. A portion of the writing integrates philosophy, theology and morality of sex.

PART 2: MASTURBATION AND PORNOGRAPHY

INTERMEZZO

Introduction

"Oh yeah, we all use to jerk off as kids. Sure, we all outgrew that stage as soon as we got our first piece of ass."

"I read *Playboy* and *Penthouse* for the articles. Once in a while I glance at *Men's Exercise*, not to look at the bulging bikini briefs, but to check out articles on fitness and health. *Cosmopolitan* and the Sunday paper lingerie ads are of passing interest, I would never think of taking them into the bathroom."

Of course not, we've outgrown such purulent interests when we got our first piece of ass in high school. Maybe some of us haven't outgrown this part of our sexuality.. The language is a little raw, but stay with it, we know that deep down you like to be talked to like this. A lot of this narrative was written some 10 or more years ago when I was a bachelor and reflects a stream of consciousness.

The Gatorade Bottle and the Carrot

Boy, do I feel horny. Everybody is gone, I've got the place to myself and am completely alone. No kids, no wife, nothing until Tuesday when they all come back. I look in the refrigerator and see the frozen lasagna she left. Not hungry, at least not now, I'm just horny. My last feeble attempt at getting some from wifey was met with little enthusiasm.... she made some comment that "is that all I think about? I'm more than just a hole for you to stick it in...etc." I'm going out.

Every time I go to the Union Newsstand, I feel a little sheepish. I hate to ogle at the used porno magazine section, but all the new stuff are covered with black plastic, no see through packaging. Use to be really good stuff I could get into, like XXX, now it's mostly soft porn like *Hustler.* Oh well, better than nothing. I'd like to look at the gay section, but all the other guys are checking out regular stuff, except for that one dude looking at *Blue Boy.* I think I'll just grab a cellophane pack of gay mags, and another pack of girlie stuff and get out of here. The Chinese fellow at the cash register, packs my purchases in a black plastic bag, just big enough to accommodate my delicious purchases. On the way out, a rather evil looking guy mumbles something like, "eat me." I'm not sure he said that, but that's what it sounded like.

Why did that sound so enticing? I remember a novel I read where the girl calls down from a tree to an irate neighbor "Eat me raw,

mister." Sticks in my mind, as I hurry home to get something to stick in my hand. I can't wait, my dick is getting hard.

Home again, and a short stop by the refrigerator to fill a glass with ice. A generous portion of scotch follows and off to the bedroom. Oh, I forgot to mention, I'd given up smoking, but stopped by the Circle K to pick up a pack of Marlboros.

I need a few more things before I prop up the pillows and strip to my skivvies. First I place the dresser mirror so I can see between my legs when I'm on the bed. I really like to look at my swollen dick and bouncing balls when I'm gently stroking it while looking at some tantalizing cleavage, pulsating slits or bung holes. I saved a Gatorade bottle and have selected a carrot about the size of a young man's dick, not too small and not to large. A carrot to substitute for a butt plug or dildo, because I couldn't have such things laying around for the wife or kids to ask about. "Daddy, can I borrow your dildo?" No, I don't need that.

Almost ready, my dick is growing hard in anticipation. I take out a small jar of Vaseline and place it on the night stand next to the little black bag. I remove my shirt, throw it on the floor, let my trousers drop, sit on the bed, pull of my socks, I had already kicked off my loafers. My dick feel semi-hard underneath my briefs, I give it a gently tug, it feels just great. I lay back, take a pull of scotch and light a cigarette. oh boy, this is going to be great.

I take my first pack of books and tear away the cello packaging revealing an old issue of *Hustler*. I gingerly leaf through it and glance at the gorgeous cunts on display, I give my bone a gentle tug. The other girlie magazines are just as blatant, but the "girls"

looked a little tough, sort of drugged, their eyes are messed up somehow.

I'm not sure I want to beat off just yet, and I feel an attraction towards looking at the gay male mags I purchased. The first one is *Rump,* and as soon as I crack the cover, I'm looking at a choice crack. A beautiful young ass with compact pink balls and cock dangling beneath a very desirable asshole. My dick goes ridged and pops out of my briefs.I pull them off and throw them on the floor, admiring my swollen and lovely looking cock in the mirror. Why, it's just a big and thick as the boys in *Rump.* I stoke it and grab my balls. Hmmmm, feels so good. Much better than trying to pump my reluctant wife.

After we turn a few more pages, I fantasize sucking a fat swollen cock, and grab my penis pretending one of these Adonis is sucking me off as I put his cock in my mouth and lick it, suck it and wait for it to vibrate into orgasm, spouting man cream into my mouth and face. I'm just about ready to cum, but back off. I want to be fucked in the ass. I look intently on a large frontal view of a pulsating dick, and dip my cleverly designed carrot in the Vaseline. I slowly insert it in my rectum, every so gently. I'm surprised at how easily it goes in. Maybe I really could enjoy anal intercourse with a man. I shove it in about 6 or 7 inches, it feels so good. I can feel my sphincter close on the fantasy fuck, and unusual deeper muscles close on the make believe dick, or maybe it's my prostate responding, something deep inside is happening and it feels great! I like looking in the mirror and seeing the carrot slide in and out.

Now I'm ready to fuck one of these pictures. Ah, here's a nice one, the young lad is bent over with his jock strap around his knees. He's spreading his buns inviting me to slip my head gently in his

asshole. I put a little Vaseline around the rim of my Gatorade bottle. I held in under the hot water a little while ago and it's still warm. Oh yes, I had put my carrot in the microwave to give it a bit of warmth. Looking intently at the young backside entrance, I place the Gatorade bottle over my dick and thrust forward, imaging it to be the tight asshole I'm staring at. It is tight. I wonder if Gatorade made the neck on their products so much like a tight cunt or asshole on purpose? The warmth of the water treatment and the lub of the Vaseline do their job and I'm in.

I switch my fantasy back to getting blown, so I squeeze the bottle and it act just like I would imagine someone sucking on my dick. The pressure is very pleasing, and as I squeeze, my dick pops out. Well, all my senses are aroused, and I can't put it off any longer, I grab my dick and begin to pump it fiercely. Up and down, up and down, I look in the mirror, my balls are bouncing mightily. I glance at a particularly erotic picture I had selected beforehand that I would cum on, it's a picture of a young lad laying across the lap of another young man who is about to shove a dildo up his young chum's ass. There balls are touching. Wooosh, out comes the man cream, lots of it, on my hand, my leg, the towel I placed under my butt. I think, "it doesn't get any better than this." I look at my hand and there are little strings of cum hanging between my fingers. I'm satisfied. It was great. I know I'll wake up in a few hours, turn on the light and do it all over again.

The Seminary-Early Years, A Follow-on Reflection on Part I

This section is abit repetitious and is included because it was written as part of this 10 year old writing and includes some other thoughts of this time. Please bear with the author and skip as appropriate those thoughts that are redundant.

At the age of thirteen, I headed off for High School (9th grade) Seminary to begin studying for the Roman Catholic Priesthood. What a wondrous setting in 1500 acres of rolling northern Wisconsin hills, the gothic styled church and seminary buildings were serene and inviting, especially in September when the apple trees flourished close at hand.

Early in the morning, I could reach under a heavily laden apple tree and pull a cold and still dew covered "snowball" variety. They were small, juicy and pure white on the inside.

The discipline was ridged, up at 5:00 am for a full day of Latin, English, Math, History and other typical high school courses. Study halls, recreation and prayer filled in the non-classroom hours with a "lights out" at 9:00.

I didn't have much trouble with "no girls" and the idea of the irrevocable vow of celibacy during the 9th and 10th grades. When I became a Junior, I began experiencing nightly hard-ons with accompanying erotic images. As I drifted off to sleep, I would

begin to rub myself against the mattress, or unintentionally fondle myself. Frequently I would ejaculate.

This was matter for the confessional, but as I was only half-awake, there was little if any culpability. As a matter of fact, by the time Senior year came about, I was rather enjoying the event, and was glad there was no sin attached to it because I wasn't able to give full consent of the will due to my semi-conscious state.

Almost unbelievably, I remained "pure", no intentional masturbation for the entire nine years of seminary life. This also included summer vacations. Nightly occurrences were frequent and sometimes a little questionable as to how awake I was.

What finally happened, was the Disciplinarian at the major seminary counseled me to leave, as he thought this nocturnal habit might cause me some problems later on, and that perhaps I wasn't suited for a life of celibacy.

I joined the Navy. You know, this was back in the 60's and I really don't recall running into one gay priest, seminarian or even a gay sailor. Of course I wasn't looking for them.

My bunkie onboard ship turned out to be gay. He was always being "surprised" by a unforeseen gay occasion or approach. I just thought he had bad luck.

I tried to stay chaste while in the Navy, with the exception of a few portside romps with the ladies for hire. Although I did find the shipboard newspaper with the featured pin-ups a cause for a hard-on. My fellow officers lounged around in their bunks and seemed to have an ample supply of soft porn which they confiscated from the enlisted. Once in a while I would slip into a beat-off session

with what available porn I could find. No sooner done, and I would feel really guilty having committed a mortal sin. I would seek a priest for confession at the earliest I could do so.

This syndrome continued for years. Even after marriage. Sex in marriage was marginal. It surprising how eager the bride to be was, but then after "I do", I got mostly "I don't".

So, back to the hands on masturbating next to the corpse, occasionally the corpse would move, but not in any kind of inviting fashion. Like the old joke, while a couple where having sex, the husband asks: "Honey, did I hurt you?" The wife responds: "No, why?'"

Husband: "You moved."

The bi-sexual, or gay and straight attraction started maybe 20 years ago. Always by way of the imagination. Supported by XXX movies and magazines, the fantasies were very enjoyable and very guilt ridden. I often remarked after a particularly steamy session that "It just doesn't get any better than this!" I never did have an actual gay sexual encounter, and am a little afraid of it. Also the idea of kissing another man is not appealing, neither is licking his crack. Sucking his cock is appealing, and fucking him in the ass is also appealing.

I think I would like to be fucked, but by a man with a slender penis, nothing that would cause pain. I'd like to do it without a rubber for the full effect, but that really scares me.

Viginity and Booze

We had a neat group of guys and gals at the CYO (Catholic Youth Organization), and this outfit put together a "Dude Ranch" weekender bender. Maryann came with me and was she hot. A nice little Italian girl that just loved to smooch and make out. Of course, being just out of the seminary and still a celibate (yes, a virgin at 22), I was still in the kissy-face stage of my sexual development, hadn't even copped a feel. Well, a quart of Ballentine scotch, yes, they still had quarts, not 750ml, or liters, but good old solid quarts of booze, accompanied Maryann and I to the dude ranch. We arrived Friday evening and immediately started square dancing. I poured a generous scotch on the rocks and off we went. After working up a pretty good sweat, (when you're young and celibate, sweating is OK, you don't seem to smell badly) Maryann and I disappeared under a nearby pine tree with our bottle of Ballentine. We rolled around in the grass, hugged and kissed, nice long juicy kisses, but I still didn't venture a hand up here dress. I didn't feel her up, that would come later.

My first sexual encounter was Saturday in Maryann's room. We were laying on her bed, fully clothed, smooching away. I unsnapped her jeans and slid my hand down her very small and virginal crotch and let my finger do the walking. I put one finger in her vagina and slowly finger fucked her. I enjoyed this immensely, never having felt a cunt before. I put in another finger, boy, was she ever tight. We did this for probably a couple of hours, she never touched me

and I had a rod that could have supported the the Empire State building.. But you know, I really wasn't focused on myself, my attention was entirely on Maryann and her lovely lips, both above and below.

I felt guilty, and because it was Saturday, sought out a church with a confessional open for business. As luck would have it, there was a small Catholic Church nearby and I unloaded my guilt ridden soul. I promised to avoid "the occasion of sin" and try again to be pure. Maryann hung out with her girl friends and I avoid her. She must have felt a little guilty too, as she was stand offish. Well, St. John (that's me) finished the weekend and we jumped into our friend's car, Maryann and I in the back seat along with several others and headed back home to Schenectady. Maryann and I in the back seat became re-acquanited with long, luscious kisses. That girl truly taught me how to kiss!

That summer I went to Newport RI as an officer candidate for the US Navy. Maryann wrote me daily, little cute cards, passionate love letters of desire. She was one hot chick, and helped me, the former seminarian, get through a tough military course of which I knew zilch. I would even put my spats on backwards for marching drill and hurt my hand doing gun maneuvers with an M1 WWII heavy duty rifle. But Ah, there was an interlude.

Maryann and her friend Maureen, were able to conn Maryann's mother into letting them drive their 1952 faded green Dodge to New York city. I had a friend, Arnold, who lived in the city and gave me a weekend lift to meet Maryann. It was wonderful. I was dressed in my Navy blue midshipman uniform, complete with snazzy white combination cap. The girls really go for a dude in uniform, especially a 6'2" slender virginal dude. We walked and

talked, toured NY, took the Staten Island ferry for 15 cents each. A lovely, inexpensive diner of spaghetti at a side walk Manhattan outdoor cafe set the mood bed time.

Maryann and I chastely slipped under the covers with our underwear on. We were quiet, as Maureen was in the bed next to us, probably pretending to be asleep, but more than likely being all ears. We kissed and she lead my stick prick to the lips of her very small cunt. I couldn't penetrate. It was like trying to stick it in a coke bottle, just wouldn't fit. I literally popped out, not having gotten past the first set of lips. Oh well, I thought it was God's will and besides, I didn't have a rubber and never have fucked anybody anyway. So I left NY with my virginity in tact, but an older and wiser man. My dick did eventually go down before I returned to base.

What's all this have to do with drinking? Not much, I don't even think I had a drink in my NY affair with Maryann. I think drinking started to influence my life, both my married life, limited sex life and business world when I turned 40. My evenings were mostly spent in the library, a room I finished off into a secluded den just off the family room, reading, listening to the stereo an sipping fine beverages from my "field bar." This was a wooden piece of furniture that supported a decanter, crystal glasses to match and had wooden sides cut out to hold one's favorite booze. In my case, it was George Dickel bourbon, Dewars scotch, and some brandy. These I sipped as my family sat in the next room watching TV. I would retire and find my spouse asleep. I would nudge her looking for some sex and get a "don't bother me" kind of response. I a semi-coma I would start to masturbate, trying not to let the gentle motion wake her, I'd be embarrassed. I think she knew what I was doing though, as occasionally she would grab my hand, not my dick, to stop the process. Just lovely.

I found that I was getting more and more morose, and communication was at a virtual standstill. Oh, I was cheery and bouncy in the morning, getting coffee for the wife, delivering it with a freshly picked gardenia from our yard. She would light a cigarette and continue primping, I might get a semi-smile. Upon our mutual departing for work I might be offered a cheek to peck. Big fucking hairy deal!

We separated after almost 20 years of marriage, most of those as brother and sister who didn't get along too well. I was so horny I could shit. In two months I dated 25 girls and couldn't get to first base. I had a hardon especially for a twenty-something who was an artist and smoked pot. I could have died to get her in bed, but she said she didn't have that special click for me. Back to *Hustler* and the hand jobs. I didn't really have any inclination to homosexual fantasies at this time, I was strictly heterosexual, or trying to be, about the only sex I was experiencing was with Merry Hand.

Finally Ginger entered. Or rather I entered Ginger, a lovely blond who hadn't had a date for over a year. She was down on men, but for some reason, took to me and wanted to be fucked really bad. I think it was the ride on my motorcycle, the attention I paid to her and the gently squeezes on her thigh as we motored the North Georgia mountains. She literally, took me to bed, sucked me and pounced her red hot cunt on my really eager cock. She screamed, "Ahh, oh, I'm coming all over you!" And she did...wow. It was the first time I was had a women since I was married. I was one of those faithful dudes. If that cunt I was married to, did this even once, things might have been different. She was just a man emasculating, armored plate, frozen cunt that had her own agenda and it didn't include *moi*.

Still not much in the way of booze. I had cut down considerably. My roomy who I was sharing an apartment with, did a good job on the vodka. I thought *he* was drinking too much. His health, job and finances all went into the shiter. Not a happy life. He died.

I didn't notice my drinking becoming a steady item until it reached a pretty consistent six to eight drinks a day. This is also when I noticed a desire of homosexual pornography and masturbation in preference to normal heterosexual sex and female porno. The effect of alcohol tends to isolate me, make me think of my dick and throw me into intemperate desire of sensual pleasures, avoiding work or any kind of mental activity other than leafing through porn books. I loss a lot of time and energy. I wack off so much that I'm exhausted and don't feel good. Everything is a bother and effort. People irritate me. I have little interest in anything, I'm bored, really bored. I have just enough energy to get to the pity pot.

Drinking Re-evaluated

I happened upon a book: *Moderate Drinking* by Audrey Kishline. I was so impressed with it, I actually gave up alcohol for 45 days and wrote a letter to *Newsweek* relating my experience. The letter succinctly tells it all and I'll enclose it for your reading pleasure.

"The Big 6/8, six the easy way, 8 the hard way! A common call heard at he craps tables in Vegas. For me it was the number of drinks I was daily consuming. Not just carefully poured out shot glass drinks, but robust poured from the 1.75 plastic liter of $9.88 Vodka until about and add a dash of Cranberry Juice Cocktail for color and flavor.

I'd have about two or three of these manly Cape-Codders when getting home from work. I'd change into tennis togs and meet the guys for a set of doubles. Larry brought the beer, so we'd have a few during and after the match. Dinner would follow preceded by a Gimlet or two, and them either beer or wine with dinner. A little relaxation after dinner, a scotch while reading my book. Gosh, I must have passed out in my chair, it's 2:30 am.

The Big 6/8 was starting to increase to more like 10 or 12 drinks a day, which seemed to be becoming shorter. My energy level and consciousness departed with my last toddy for the body around 8:30 p.m..

Any book I read about discerning if I'm an alcoholic I read with a bias? Not me! I don't want to go to AA, I can handle it, I seldom have a hangover, I'm not late for work, it's just that I don't seem to have the energy I once had, and I have very little patience. I'm angry a lot and my personality seems to be changing. Also my eyes are seldom clear, bright and shiny, the whites are always red-veined and the rest of the eye has a rather glazed, dull look. My problem solving abilities and memory seem to be less than what they once were.

Well after reading this fine little book of 166 pages, I took the first step and admitted I had a bad habit and hoped it was not too late to do something about it on my own.

As it turned out, it wasn't too late. Giving up the booze was a lot harder than giving up smoking. I humbly admit I use to smoke like a furnace, anything that burned found its way into my mouth. But you know, words are powerful. One day a friend of mine asked me if I inhaled my cigars. I gave the usual response: "Oh, sometimes." He replies: "Your lungs must look like cork." I quit shortly thereafter, and found that there is life after giving up smoking.

I try to drink moderately now, but if I'm not careful, the Big 6/8 comes right back with a vengeance. Drinking may have to go the way of smoking unless I can control it better.

To conclude all this, let me say that drinking makes me horny, sometimes, if I don't pass out. During my 45 days of abstinence, I didn't buy any porn or beat off. It just wasn't much of an interest.

Update on the Drinking Deal, or Ordeal:

As of this writing I have given up all alcohol, except for my Old Spice Cologne. Hey, it's just too much aggravation. I pretty much was sticking to wine and beer...oh yeah. I had a 5 litter wine-in-the –box in the fridge...I could dose it out like water. Plus 3 liter bottles of White Zinfadel, Cabernet, and maybe some Cream Sherry. Water? Very little, if I was thirsty I'd pour a tumbler of wine.

Also, I would hide a small travel bottle of vodka to spike my cans of Fresca when in the garage. Truly hooked, addicted and feeling the results of wasted time, less amorous toward my wife, because of the obsession of porno, which a few glasses of wine would direct me to the internet and wacking off. You know, www. Whatever could very well stand for whackey-whackey-whack. Especially with binary newsgroup involvement.

I have found through the years that the computer is just like having a hard-core porno store right next to your house. All free, all delights from the youngest to the oldest, to bi, trans, homo, lesbian and whatever in between or gross sex is depicted. All downloadable onto a CD and presto! Drop trousers, put on slide show and whack off to hundreds of images. Truly most addictive and obsessive.

So the program now is to give up the booze which is a direct link to one's Johnson (Dick, penis) and whacking off. The next thing

is to format the library of porn images and delete the newsgroup set-up. Hard? Very hard.

This has been a little sidetrack from the "intermezzo" portion and we will now return to it. Nevertheless, let me add a current update: I am a recovering alcoholic. Read where Audrey Kisline went to jail for vehicular homicide involving drunkenness and realized, moderation management wouldn't get it for me either.

I didn't attend AA, but resolved never to drink alcohol again. It's been several months now and I think I can do it, just like stop smoking years ago. It's harder to give up drinking, but then non-alcoholic beers are OK.

And now a return to writings of yesteryear:

The Used Rubber in the Bathroom Wastebasket

There it lies, full of cum, nowhere to go. I look in the mirror at my limp dick and reflect on the pleasure I had of jacking off using a rubber.

Damn! It felt good, but why do I feel guilty. Isn't my dick just a joy stick to give me release and pleasure?

A theological pause that occurred during this writing period:

I think about something I read in the Bible, in the beginning of the Bible about the first man and woman, Adam and Eve.

It all started when the Awesome One, the Creator said: "LET THERE BE!"

And there was being

A process of coming evolved. The stage was set, everything was in order, magnificent in variety and interdependence, only the dependence was without choice: everything moved , lived and had its being in the SOURCE.

Freedom came in the person of a man (man is used here as inclusive to include woman), destined to freely choose a relationship of love with God, the Creator. This relationship would be to freely choose *to receive* grace (grace understood to be God's gift of Himself), to be filled and to share with other men and all creation the gifts of Divine Love through caring and thoughtful service. The *choice* was man's to make.

Another creation that was gifted with freedom was a pure spirit that tradition calls an angel. By God's design, the angel had an irrevocable choice of God (good) or Anti-God (evil). The mission of opposition to God was granted and evil became spiritually incarnated... not unforeseen, but still an embarrassment.

The radical choice is ours today. We can choose life or death on a daily basis until death makes our decision irrevocable.

Back to the core of yesteryear writing:

Masturbation

A little diddy from Jr. High School days:
"Last night, I stayed up late to masturbate,
it felt so good, I knew it would.
Last night, I stayed up late to masturbate,
it felt so good, I knew it would.
Pull it with my hand, tug it with my feet
this is really neat.
Slam it on the floor,
wrap it around the door.
Some people like to fuck,
but I'd rather use my hand." (Sung to the tune of "Stout
   Hearted Men")
Oh sure, as kids we use to jerk off, but most of us have
   outgrown it. Yeah, right.
Did I feel guilty about this as a kid? There I was, sitting on the toilet
seat, fondling myself until I had an erection, and then gliding my
hand up and down my penis feeling the exquisite sensation until
I ejaculated. Boy, did that ever feel good. But there was a sense of
shame. I would flush the toilet so that if anyone was listening, they
would think I went number two, instead of beating off

Why the sense of same? Genital excitation by means of using the
hands for either the male or female is a normal tendency. Genital
excitation to the point of orgasm is an extremely pleasurable intense

sensation and sought after in many contexts. Visual titillation of pornography, video or just scantily clad individuals of either sex can start a process of masturbation.

Another philosophical/theological pause:

In his book, *In Pursuit of Love*, V.J. Genovesi asks if the action of masturbation ..."accurately express the fact that a person's fundamental relationship with God and others is being deliberately and intentionally curtailed?" The ethical and spiritual principle involved here is the self focus on pleasure to the exclusion of others, and possibly to the exclusion of God if the intention is sexual worship above all else. Is it preferring the created to the creator, in other words, is the focus of lust to the exclusion of what may be right or wrong, pleasing or displeasing to God?

Scripture in the Epistles of St. Paul gives insight to the mind and heart of God, when it gives examples of men and women who have dedicated their bodies to sexual pleasures of impurity and have chosen these pleasures against the will of God.

The sexual urge is important in bringing the sexes together for love of each other and obeying the will of God in working with him in procreation. Like all passions, i.e. anger, guilt, fear and worry, the passion of lust must be controlled by wisdom, love, prudence, temperance, justice and the courage of the grace of God to make the effort. Unfortunately, the effort is difficult, and the yielding to the passion of lust very easy and tempting.

A brief addition:

Basically man's nature tends to entrophy, that is, tends to the lease path of resistance. Given the choice between sensual pleasure and

the gratification of sexual release, man naturally tends to obey his dick. Higher intellectual functions are placed on hold as the reptilian part of the brain seeks to get off. .

XXX

The first really XXX movie I saw was in black and white, and the guy wore black socks. It was shown on an old Bell & Howell movie projector, using 16mm film and I viewed it at a Naval Reserve meeting, would you believe it? I could not believe it when the screen projected a cunt filled in with a pumping engorged prick, sliding back and forth amid bouncing balls, and not the kind you follow when doing a sing-a-long. The panting in the audience was only surpassed by the moans on the screen.

I visited a new XXX store the other day. They've been outlawed here for over ten years and I guess some entrepreneurs are going to give it another go, especially since the nude dancer establishments have proliferated without much hassle. What caught my eye upon entering was a display of anal expanders. It is a device shaped like a butt plug, only made of rubber and expandable by squeezing air from a connected tube. It looked like it might be titillating, shoving that plug up my anus and pumping it up. I bet the sensation is neat, and could be all the more fun if some young guy was doing the pumping as a prelude to lubbing up my asshole for receiving his young cock.

I sauntered by the XXX Gay mags, and reminisced how I use to ogle them in the past, with there slick covers displaying guys sucking each other off, cum splashed on their young faces. Since

all the mags were sealed with plastic bags, I could just imagine the inside pages showing graphic rimming and sodomizing, my dick was getting hard. The high price, ranging from about $13 to $40 began to soften my dick. I looked at the for rent in private viewing room videos and wish I had the time and the courage to rent, sit and enjoy.

I rented a gay flick in Florida once, gosh it was lengthy. This guy comes over to another guy's pad and gets right down to eating his asshole out, I mean big time munching. I wish I could lick my supper plate as clean as he lick this guys butt hole. After that he starts a slow languorous fuck. It goes on interminably, with the guy being fucked having his legs over this other guy's shoulders. The screen fills with a hot pole being shoved up and asshole, right to matching balls. My dick really got hard, and I wanted to join the countless thousands who shot their wads all over the booth I was sitting in and availed themselves of the paper towel roll. I resisted , though, didn't want to commit a mortal sin, I was just curious, that's all. I left the place a little sheepishly and rather exhausted, the music alone on these videos really wears you out.

I returned to my motel, dropped trousers and wacked off, couldn't help it, the images were just too strong. Thumpa, thumpa, thumpa.... wooooshh.

Boy, I like dirty movies. I would really like to have a collection at home on my VCR, but I'm too chicken. What if I should die and my kids find XXX gay movies on my shelf? It would be awful. Also, I still have scruples about masturbating with pornography and don't consider it entirely guilt free, which is the next topic of our conversation.

Dress Fit to Kill

Just had a shower and am a little bored. Nothing to do, really and no place to go exactly. Standing in front of the mirror and looking at myself, what a lovely cock! Think I'll touch it, hmmm. I've a long, thin brown shoelace, think I'll tie under my balls and around the shaft of my lovely penis. Hmmmmm, that feels good. I'm getting a little turgid, I like it.

Some time ago, I stopped by Joe Bikinis shop on Piedmont. It's not there anymore, but it use to supply the snap off bikinis for the nude dancers, both for the girls and boys. Just before they closed, I was digging through a "sale" box of goodies and came up with a male stripper bikini, a thong with a pouch in brilliant hues of chartreuse, pink and green. I asked Matt, the young clerk, if this was me, he agreed it was. I also found a gay man's bathing suit in hot orange with a little yellow tag on the rear which read "Pan Dulce", which I think is French for "All Sweet". Matt thought this was me also. The list price for these treasures came to about $50. They were on sale for five dollars each, I bought both fantasies.

The bathing suit reminded me of a visit I paid to a gay apartment complex located in Ansley. It was about noon, and I was traveling by the pool on my way to the rental office. I was working for a sign company at the time, and I was going to call on the Office Manager and inquire if they might need our services. As I drove by the pool, I notice about a dozen young men lounging about, working on

their tans and erections. One in particular caught my eye. He was lean and blond, probably late teens or early twenties. He had on a swim suit similar in design and cut to the one I purchased at Joe's. He was chatting with a dude, combing his long blond hair in a sort of feline way, and thrusting his hips out which outline his long tool lovingly displayed in tight spandex. My dick started to grow hard. I parked, and moved to a picnic table with some paperwork and occupied myself with writing, all the while studying the gay pool manscape. There were a lovely assortment of buns. Blond boy was gesturing to his nipples and cock to his attentive pool pal. Another Adonis had stepped out of the pool and was drying off. I'd like to suck him off, if he asked me. He put on a pair of shorts, much like a girl does when she leaves the pool and doesn't want to display her lovely buns and snatch barley covered by a spandex thong. In the process, his penis bobs up and down before disappearing behind the zipper of his shorts. These thoughts are making my cock grow hard as I continue in my boredom, in front of the mirror after my shower.

Think I'll put on both the thong, and the "Pan Dulce", hmmmm looks great. My swollen, tied up cock bulges even better that the young poolside studs. I sit on my bed and carefully pull on a pair of black pantyhose, which I acquired one Halloween for a costume. I went as a cheerleader, and enjoyed the sensation of dressing as a girl, I do have attractive, hairless long legs. I have to be careful in putting on the pantyhose, for they tear easily. Boy, would I like to tear into some young boy-ass. I'm getting hot and want to fuck a male asshole. My cock is throbbing and I begin to undress in front of the mirror. First the black pantyhose, is your cock or clit aroused? I peel off the layers of spandex and untie the shoelace around my long, beautiful penis and cup my balls gently. Ever try

fucking yourself? It's not as hard as trying to suck yourself off, but just as impossible for the average 6 to 8 inch cock. In order to suck yourself, or jam your tool up your own ass, I would think you need about 10 inches of prod. Anyway, I take my penis, which has lessen somewhat in erection and rub it between my legs, between my right thigh, and testicle, gently slipping it toward the rear. With a little effort I can almost put the head of my dick in my ass. It's close, I can feel it touch and almost insert. I'm getting really hot now, I turn around and look in the mirror, I see my balls, my hand thrusting my dick very close to the orifice of my anus. Darn, wish I had a couple of more inches, I'd be home, baby. Right up my ass! I settle for a gentle masturbation just between by balls and asshole. It's a tender spot and both my dickhead and the spot enjoy the steamy sensation. Pow, a juicy blop of jizz spurts out on the spot and feels warm and sticky. Guess I'll have to take another shower, if I'm not too weak.

Was Boredom the Culprit?

It's a funny thing about masturbation, the urge seems to come on strong when:

- I'm bored.
- I've had a hard day, stressed out, and want a drink, smoke and relax.
- I'm alone, and have to do something mental that I don't want to do, like required reading for work or school, juggling a schedule to accommodate interests in which I have none.
- Biologically, the day before my herpes acts up, or some other not understood cause.
- Drinking, which is definitely a trigger.
- I just have an urge to buy porno.

If I'm with people and doing something interesting, yanking out my dick and jacking off would be an inconvenience. But if I'm bored, *isolated*, alone and have some porn, I get hot, stroke it and enjoy a great release. But do I really *feel* good about it afterward?

Woody Allen, a great satirist and actor, once said that "the difference between dying alone and having sex alone is that people don't laugh at the former." Wacking off is a solitary, self-centered pleasure, even it is done by another. Is the only love it expresses is self-love? Perhaps self-love is OK, if it allows a diffusion of love to and for another person, and not a thing. Love of things still puts

us square into ourselves and self gratification. Selfishness seems a bit lifeless, useless, stale and tomorrowless.

Ooppsie, another Phi/Theo comment:

Aha, a clever acronym developed by a friend of mine, Fr. Val LeFrance, an Indian of great stature. To wit:

L: lifeless
U: useless
S: staleness
T: tomorrowless

What is the difference between LOVE and LUST?

LOVE is patient. *LUST* wants it now, like in Redneck foreplay: "On your back, bitch."

LOVE seeks others, shares, wants the best for another. *LUST* doesn't give a shit.

LOVE gives life, perhaps new life, a baby. *LUST* might have a "love baby" (what a misnomer) that is a problem. "Wham, bam, thank you mam, have an abortion."

LOVE is something of value. LUST is fleeting as Shakespeare has said: *"Tyrannical lust, unreasoned hunted, no sooner had than unreasoned hated."*

Back to mainstream:

Paper Dolls

Cutting out paper dolls, my oh my, what a guy! Sometimes, I get horny and feel a little guilty about buying soft porn such as *Mandate, Playguy* or *Honcho* and settle for a copy of *Playgirl*. Mostly, the guys are in a limp or semi erect state, but there are more pictures of partially clad studs and they don't looks so weird. The regular soft porn mags as mentioned above all seem to have guys that look a little dumb or mental, you know, like a retard kind of look. Their eyes look a little weird. Also, if I'm buying a cello pack of older issues, the thought comes to me that most of these "models" are probably dead of AIDS by the time I'm ogling their bodies. The lovely dicks and assholes I'm drooling over are probably buried.

So, I'm getting off paging through the issue of *Playgirl*, and some poses are more stimulating than other photos. In particular I like bun shots, so I get a pair of scissors and cut out those pictures that really turn me on, and scotch tape them to my mirror. Boy, this is hot stuff! The idea occurs to me to cut this guy out with a hardon and insert his dick in another rear picture of himself and make a little ass fucking working cut out. As I activate it I think how clever I am. It doesn't beat the *hard core porno*, but it beats laying out $20 to$40+ for such as that. Besides, once beat jacked off, it doesn't matter if I used even *Cosmopolitan* for visual delights, it's over. You see, I haven't purchased expensive porno videos, or relatively expensive hard core porn, because after awhile, I feel so

guilty that I have to try to start being chaste again and therefore have to clean out the closet. In other words, throw out the porn. Just like giving up drinking for awhile. Let me tell you why I do this in my next little vignette.

More soul searching...

Letting Go

I'm Roman Catholic, and still have qualms about masturbation. Oh, I've read varying opinions trying to justify occasional wacking off, but when I reach a point where I did last night, I have to throw my crutches out, go to confession, and try, try again to adopt a more disciplined life style. It's just the way I am, and it is a burden.

Last night, I opted for masturbation in preference for live sex with my girl friend. Oh yes, I've been divorced for many years and that's why I have complete liberty, or shall we say, license, to drop my trousers and pull my pud anytime I please. Even when I do have sex with her, I use her as a surrogate, and we do it doggie style, thinking of her, fantasizing that she is a man and I'm screwing her in the ass. She seems to enjoy it though, and I truly love her and am sorry I have to use this deception in order to get a hardon.

It all comes down to my sexuality and preference of using objects as a means of orgasm. Even my cutting out dicks, assholes etc. and masturbate on them indicates that I don't want sex with a person, I'd rather isolate the activity and use masturbation solely for my pleasure and release.

Well, after she went home, and I had a considerable quantity of alcohol, I dug up my recently thrown away Gatorade bottle, a hot dog which I warmed in the microwave and stripped to my nice black bikini cut briefs. I started reading porn stories, accompanied by pictures from *Rump*. I put the hot dog in some Vaseline slowly

threaded up my ass while looking at a picture of a young boy getting dildoed. The hot dog felt good, but wasn't stiff enough to really do the job. I left in partially inserted while I put the Gatorade bottle over my somewhat erect stick. I squeezed the bottle, pretending the vacuum sucking effect was some Adonis sucking me off. I had too much to drink and had difficulty in coming, but eventually I came. I looked at the small amount of cum on my hand and thought about licking a little of it to see what it tasted like. I always think about doing this before I come, but never do it afterward, except once. It tasted a little like chalk.

I passed out, and awoke a bit later only to be obsessed again with my porn and pud. What a site, trying to whack off a limp, used up prick, but the heat in my loins, urges me on...whack-a-whack-a-whack. Cum and go. Go back to sleep.

So, you see, it's time to give up the bottle, both Gatorade and Vodka, and try to get straight once again. My conscience tells me I'm over the edge and need reconciliation. You probably think I need a shrink, and maybe I do, but I can't afford the advice. So, I'll say a prayer, go to confession nd continue to cope as best I can.

Mistaken Identity

In some pornographic literature, men seem to like anal penetration. It's like they are an insatiable woman, able to receive dick after dick and yet remain ready for more. They think that getting penetrated is really super satisfying. One porno vignette I read describes the guy's lover putting an electric dildo up his ass while blowing him. He turns on the dildo and creates all kinds of jumpy, exquisite sensations from asshole to prostrate to balls and cock, which is being suck with great vigor. The suckee cums with load after load of man cream and then spreads them for his sucker to insert his prod.

Other porn describes "Shemales" those people who look and act like a woman, but when they get to the crotch, there's a penis and balls. So, is there some kind of hang up here? Has blatant forms of feminism distorted male sexuality to the point of some thinking they are both male and female, or others thinking they are transsexual? Or has the relentless search for amusement in masturbation led to fantasies that include any hole, male, female, dog or cat, chained or unchained.

Mother Theresa had an interesting message that she sent to Beijing on the occasion of the U.N. women's conference held there in 1995.

"All God's gifts are good, but they are not the same. God created all people to love and be loved, but God also created man and woman to be different.

A woman's love is one image of the love of God, and a man's love is another image of God's love. Woman and man complete each other, and together show forth God's love more fully than either can do alone. Woman and man complete each other, and together show forth God's love more fully than either can do alone.

God told us, 'Love your neighbor as yourself.' So first I am to love myself rightly, and them to love my neighbor like that. But how can I love myself unless I accept myself as God has made me? People who deny the differences between men and women deny the truth of their own identities. They cannot love themselves, and they end up sowing division between people rather than loving them."

Identity, right now I identify myself with my dick. As I'm typing this I am looking at a little picture I've framed in a small 2"x3" frame of a guy's asshole . He's spreading his cheeks and displaying a young, succulent, anus slightly ringed with hair. His balls and cock are dangling down between his legs and my cock grows hard. I'd like to whip out my dick and start beating it, imaging alternately that I'm sucking him off from below and sticking my cock up his young ass. But I'm liable to shoot cum all over my keyboard and that would be a stick mess. Also, my surrogate girl friend is coming over and if I jack off, I won't be able to do much later on, and that would be unfair to her.

As I ponder the image and practice a modicum of self-control, I reflect that there is nothing remotely resembling love in regarding an object and "making love" to it. Jacking off and making love are

not the same. Actually, using a woman as a hole is not making love either, it's jacking off using an object. You know, my 2"x3" frame is small and only shows the genitalia I'm interested in. It's an object. It could be a picture of a disassociated cunt or female asshole, although the balls and cock would be missing in most cases. I find I like boys privates as objects to girls cunts and boobs. The male body is more erotic.

By this time you may think I'm a queer. I like to think of myself as confused, and not really knowing why. Maybe for sake of saving face, I could call myself a bi-sexual, although I've never had sex with another man.

To add to this ambivalence, I would like to share some thoughts I have about homosexuality.

Again, a diversion and an essay written over 10 years ago.

The Homosexual

Consider a sexual metaphor of two becoming one through sexual intercourse. Each person retains their own identity, but during the act of sexual intercourse, the penetration of another human being by a sexual organ occurs, and at the moment of orgasm, fluids are exchanged.

Aside from the intention of the people coupling, which could be a true love for one another and a desire to become one through intercourse, or the intention could be selfish love and merely a desire to find release of passion, there is nevertheless a unity of fluids.

In the former case, i.e. the unity of true love, the sexual act may be open to the transmission of sperm to the fluids of the vagina and carried to the ovum where penetration may occur once again and the two truly become one in the conception of life and a potential human being, a child. In the latter case, consummate lust could also produce the same results, and the child paradoxically is sometimes referred to as a "love child."

To think in terms of natural and unnatural acts, we analyze what "Mother Nature" has in mind regarding the naturalness or nature of the sexual act, in other words, *what's it all about*? To what purpose is the sexual act for? Does it have meaning and purpose, or is it akin to blowing one's nose, and the resultant fluid mass having equal value, or non-value?

If we think Mother Nature as a myth without meaning, we can translate this to an unreflected life and that meaning is only personal. There is no meaning except subjective meaning, that which pleases me is the only important consideration. Masturbation is a good example of divorcing meaning from sexuality. There is not joining of fluids for the production of anything, merely the release of ejaculatory fluids into the hand, or elsewhere.

Mother Nature is, of course, a personification of nature. In the Christian-Judaic culture, nature does not stand uncreated and alone, rather it is the result of creation and a Creator (Creatoress). Christian tradition has passed on the image of Christ and his Church as bride and bridegroom. The metaphor suggests the meaning of sex as a foreshadowing of the eventuality for the unification of all creation into oneness, the harmonization of all positive and negative elements into the peace and serenity of love.

As far as same-sex intercourse is concerned, the oneness occurs metaphorically as love of another. The actual aloneness at the physical level is less than the oneness of masturbation. Women having sex together achieve orgasm and fluids may be exchanged but to what purpose other than to be combined with sweat and washed away?

Men having sexual relations are even more foreign to nature as fluids combine in the anus or oral cavity for the end result of ejection.

Male and female coupling can have as a natural result, the birth of a child. The only birth that same-sex coupling yields is death. As the metaphor of God, love and unity is expressed in the natural

purpose of sex between man and woman as a union with the truth, the Father of Truth so also does the coupling of man on man unnaturally express an untruth, a union with the Father of Lies, the evil one, the Devil. To emphasize the truthfulness of this reflection, think about the common homosexual foreplay as prelude to anal intercourse and consider how repulsive and unnatural is the "rimming" of placing a man's tongue into the anal orifice of another man with the possibility of the tongue and mouth touching and ingesting the other man's fecal matter.

At root, sexuality pervades all aspects of existence. The interpretation of the meaning of such a pervasive phenomenon has to be a true interpretation. This interpretation must be passed on to our children in a convincing manner for only then will the truth set us free.

Did Jesus Masturbate?

Was Mary, his mother, always a virgin? Did Joseph, her husband, have sexual relations with Mary? Did Jesus have sex with Mary Magdalene? Did Jesus masturbate? What does God think about sex? What part does sex play in God's plan and design of things? Is sex dirty? What about sexy thoughts, perversions, such as getting sucked off by a 6 year old girl? Or how about putting some Vaseline on a tender young boy's asshole and sticking your engorged dick fully into it? Are these products of a sick mind, or is your dick getting hard just thinking about it?

Yes, my dick is getting hard just thinking about it, but you know, there's more to life than smoking, drinking, lusting and orgasms. What? Life without these things? *Unthinkable!*

I suppose some are more inclined to sex and it's many dimensions than others. And, there are competing interests that occupy the mind and body. When one is entirely taken up with a project, an interest such as working on a car, restoring classic motorcycles, engrossed in a fascinating novel, thoughts of masturbation are nowhere in sight. It's only when one is finished being involved and is tired, or when one is thinking about a task that is a pain in the ass and he or she would rather stick hot needles in the eye than do this thing, that lustful ideas present themselves as alternatives. Perhaps even after stepping out of the shower and viewing oneself in the bathroom mirror does the idea enter the mind of playing with such

a pretty dick, or massaging those gorgeous balls and pretending that some young Adonis is standing behind you, rubbing your cock, rubbing his cock up your crack, wanting to penetrate, to fill your crack with man cream. Is your cock getting stiff, mine is.

I wonder if Jesus, after a day with the crowd, stifling, pushing in on him like we see in middle east movies, the crowds of people shouting, pushing, density, hot sweating bodies, a sea of noise and need, I wonder if Jesus, when he reclined, had some refreshment, maybe a cup of wine, I wonder if his hand involuntarily reached down and massaged his genitals?

Did Jesus catch the sight of Mary Magdalene bending over to lift or get something, and notice the curve of her hips, the smooth contour of her behind, and did he get an erection?

In the rock musical *Jesus Christ Superstar*, Mary Magdalene sings a song *I don't know how to love him*. Did she have desires for Jesus sexually? Did Jesus desire her?

Don't be offended dear heart, Jesus was truly a man, and as a man he was sexual. We are told by Scripture that he was tempted in all things, but that he did not sin. And what is sin anyway. One interpretation is that sin is a condition of unbelief, of unfaith. Basically, a condition of idolatry where the creature, refuses to acknowledge God in his or her life, and prefers the created to the Creator. Sin is a distortion.

Much of our illustrations and rather frank talk about cocks, assholes, cum etc. is probably a distortion. I don't think that jacking off in the bathroom is bringing me closer to a relationship with Jesus Christ. By the same token, I don't think that Jesus used masturbation as a means of drawing closer to his Father. I'll bet

that he had wet dreams as a boy and that like all kids probably masturbated without fully realizing how solitary sex is a distortion from sexuality that is life serving, other enhancing, holistic and a deep symbol of love and creativity.

Once realizing the dimensions of his sexuality, its purpose in God's plan and realizing the distortion and perversion that can occur by following the suggestions of the Father of Lies, the old adversary, Satan, I don't think Jesus followed the path we so often take in sensual gratification without responsibility or concern for purpose. It just doesn't seem right.

Regarding Mary, his mother and Joseph his earthly dad and guardian, I find nothing contradictory in thinking they had a great sex life and some additional children. On the contrary, celibacy and virginity are so unnatural, that I find these conditions to be as much of a distortion as frank perversity. I'm afraid I have little respect for vowed celibacy. It's about as natural as cutting off ones balls and becoming a eunuch. It's a distortion. However, if someone wants to voluntarily (not mandated) choose celibacy, perhaps this can be done without consummate narcissism and selfishness. I don't know?

Dirty Jokes

Dirty jokes are probably not erotic, just in bad taste most of the time. Some are truly funny, some are just plain rotten:

> GIRL: "Daddy, can I borrow the car tonight?"
> FATHER: "No."
> GIRL: "Oh please, Daddy, please."
> FATHER: "OK, but you'll have to suck my dick first."
> GIRL: "Oh fuck, okay, stick it in my mouth."
> GIRL: "THIS DICK TASTES LIKE SHIT!"
> FATHER: "Oopsie, sorry, I forgot. Your brother already has the car tonight."

I never got a laugh out of that "joke", most people just moaned or were embarrassed. I stopped telling it.

Movies, Past and Present

The Farmer's Daughter was a triple X movie I watched back in the 70's at the Buckhead Art Theater in Atlanta. I had a secret desire to go downtown and watch a flick at the Blue Boy, which featured gay movies, but I was too embarrassed. This was one of the last full length porno movies I watched and it was a humdinger. It started out with the farm boy lying on a bed eating a young girl's pussy, as she straddled over his face. At the same time, another girl was sucking off his beautifully shaped dick. This may have been the first time I really enjoyed looking at a young, full fleshed, engorged penis. The movie turned nasty as violence entered into it. Three hoodlums, one black, two white, invaded the farmhouse at gunpoint and forced the farmer's daughters to take it up the ass. Much moaning and groaning as they were sodomized. The scene ended with the farmer getting forcibly blown by his daughter and his wife getting screwed by their son. You can see why this left me somewhat shaken. Oh yes, there was a couple of murders during this mayhem. This, I think was the beginning of the era of sex and violence in movies.

Even less satisfying, is the experience of the then quarter peek shows. A person would select what every kinky fancy turned him on and sit in a closed booth, popping quarters into a box that activated a small screen for a few moments with XXX movies. The booth had a lot of cum shots on the wall, etc. Some of the booths provided paper towels, most didn't. I'd watch with a bonner in my

pants and finally jack myself off in my pants, hoping I wouldn't leave a big cum spot, wet, sticky and visible to all on my way out.

I didn't do this much, it felt too unclean. These places smelled bad. This was before the AIDS scare. All of these places disappeared around Atlanta before the 80's.

I did try a gay movie when I was in St. Paul, MN. It was okay, though I felt a little strange when I went into the men's room to take a leak. There was this guy sitting on a couch, also some guys hanging around the stalls, all of them looked pretty gruesome, and this was before the AIDS epidemic. I just couldn't imagine asking someone to suck me off in the toilet, or for that matter, sucking some else off sitting on the crapper. Actually, I sort of can imagine it and it makes my dick grow hard.

Hoping I wasn't gay, I sneaked into the next room where a regular heterosexual fuck scene was taking place, and found my attention was easily had. I didn't jack off in my pants though, but did enjoy a throbbing hardon.

Today's movies of soft-porn are really boring. Just a lot of faces huffing and puffing with an occasion glimpse of a bun or tit. Seldom see male genitalia or a twat. Just a lot of moans. I don't bother, and rather wish for the good old days at the Buckhead Art. They may be making a return, I noticed a sexual goods store opening on Peachtree St. just last month. The girlie show places have proliferated, so I expect the ethic patrol or vice squad may no longer be on the hunt, hence the proliferation of cunt. At one time, it was just like Broadway, with XXX movies and sex stores back to back. Oddly enough, some of these establishments were located next to Sacred Heart Cathedral on old Ivy St. I use to go

to confession at noon at Sacred Heart, and try to be chaste for a while.

Male, Female, Shemale...

What is there about talking dirty, watching sexy movies, fantasizing that is so damn yummmy, yet guilt ridden? Is it just that I'm a Roman Catholic and scrupulous, or do other non-Catholics feel the same way? I bet they do, but won't admit it.

Centerfold

Aha! Bet you thought you were going to see some skin. Nope. It's just that we are half way through this book and it's a good place to take a breath and see what we are about. We stated in the brief introduction that we are seeking truth and have as an agenda something beyond titillation and making some money from the sale of this thinly disguised porno. Let's tell a little story to illustrate a very important point in trying to overcome masturbation that has gotten out of control.

For many years, the priest in the box (Roman Catholic confessional) would always admonish me to avoid the occasion of sin, i.e. porno and *try harder.* So I would dutifully throw out my porno, which I had already done before coming to confession, say my penance, and try harder with a fresh start to avoid playing with myself. This would work for typically 6 to 8 weeks, then compulsively I'd trot down to the Newsstand and pick up a cello bag of gay porno and whack off.

It wasn't always gay literature, this didn't start until my 40's. Before I always would beat off with girlie mags. Then I got interested in both. I couldn't decide whether I preferred boys or girls, or both. Now, it's pretty much guys that turns me on. Although I still enjoy looking at females, there bodies are certainly beautiful, but seldom do they make my dick grown hard. I guess it's the transition from true love of another sexually, to just wanting the solitary splendor of

pulling the pork that makes masturbation desirable. Sex objectified, isolated and enjoyed through the senses and imagination in a nice irresponsible, immature safe fashion seems available and fun, wacka-wacka-wacka(www).

But the story:

There once was a gent who was going to Detroit. He packed a map in his briefcase, and when he arrived in Detroit, to his chagrin, he had packed a map of Chicago! No matter how *hard he tried*, he could not find the street he was looking for by using the map he packed. He then thought, I'll just have a positive attitude about this. So what if I can't find the street, I just do something else, go someplace else, what does it matter. I'll find the place next trip, etc. etc. As one can see without the right map, the actions of trying harder and the mind-set of positive attitude are of little value and don't get the job done. He needs the right road map to arrive at where he wants to be. Perhaps it's the same with overcoming hedonistic masturbation that can occur at any age, but seems to be particularly attractive as one approaches mid-life, you know, the Dirty Old Man syndrome. The harder I try, the more obsessed I become with beating off. I can adopt a positive attitude about the thing, but I'm just kidding myself, because if I have that book of boy's butts stashed away in my closet, I'll be looking at it again with the usual results of www. What I really need is a different map, a different perspective on the act.

I've tried to desensitize myself by hanging a rather erotic picture of a lovely strawberry blonde bending over a Porsche with a wrench. She's wearing a tight, revealing jumper, cut just above her firm cheeks, showing just a hint of soft down. Her lovely hair is highlighted and she is wearing no hose and white spike heels. This

use to make my dick grow hard, but after constant exposure, I grew use to it, and now I look at it admiringly and without a hardon. I'm trying this with a small framed picture of a young lad spreading his cheeks, showing his sphincter and lightly downed balls and tip of his cock, as he bends over. Now this makes my dick grow hard writing about it, but in actual practice, I have this framed picture on my bathroom sink, and look at it when I'm there. I judiciously put it in the vanity under the sink when I'm not there, as guests may think it a bit weird. I find that as I grow accustom to this most erotic gay pose, I am beginning to be desensitized to it. I've thrown out my other porn, because I know as I flip rapidly through many color pictures of naked men, I'll want to fantasize and jack off.

The perspective, or new horizon that I'm trying to adapt is one of harmony and balance in nature. I'm trying to approach the objectification of sex and the lust of unrestrained passion with a world view of this is really immature and not an adult activity that allows me to think of others, love others, be a mature Christian adult.

When it comes to sin, I don't think it's so much the action itself, but the mind-set that prompts and commits to the action. For example, premeditated murder is a more grievous offense that a murder committed in the heat of passion. Still the action of murder is objectively wrong, a distortion so to speak, because you distorted another's existence into non-existence, but the enormity of the sin is the subjective adherence to it, the commitment of self to the act, you really wanted to blow this person's brains out, thought about it, planned it and executed it without regard for anything else.

Masturbation is a habit, like any other habit. It's almost like smoking. Nicotine triggers a chemical function in the brain that

says: "This feels good, let's do it again." Same with orgasms, or the anticipation of orgasms. Let's face it, we'll all have sexual desires until we are dead. True, some people are walking death, and probably haven't had a hardon in years, but these souls are the exception. It's a lot more effective to handle sexuality, our needs and desires from a calm world view of maturity and the realization that trying harder to avoid jacking off only excites to obsession. We do have some help in creating this world view, and this help is called a gift of God. It's the topic of our next chapter and it's called *grace.*

Aha, more phil/theo musings.

Grace

Before the dawn of time, there existed Existence. This existence always was and always will be, it is eternal, all powerful the uncaused cause of all that has being.

How do we know this as fact? We don't. We are not made certain about the existence of this phenomenon we name *GOD* through empirical data. We have only the Bible (inspired, revealed truths), tradition and our own intuition to guide us in our belief in God. Intuitively, there seems to be something inside of us that tells us that there is a God, and that this God is a Supreme Being who created the universe and us.

By definition, creation means to make something out of nothing. Existence has to have a cause, it has to be brought into being. We postulate a pre-existing being to give being, and this is God. It is difficult to find a true atheist, one who denies God's existence. Rather we find agnostics, those who aren't sure, and we find those who would rather ignore God's existence and pursue their own agenda of independence and self-sufficiency. Even the atheist, in trying times or in moments of fear, will call out to a Supreme Being out of need. It seems to be part of human nature to desire God. Neediness seems to be genetic.

Let's examine human nature. We can observe our procreation in which in a marvelous manner, sperm and ovum are united and cellular division proceeds, bringing forth a human. just as all life

on this planet, Earth, had to have an initial cause, the production of something form nothing, so too, there had to come into being the first man and woman. Because of our reflection on the nature of existence, we can postulate that the first man and woman were created by God.

What kind of nature would God bestow? Would it reflect His nature? (I will refer to God as He, and use capital letters for clarity. It is understood that "He" is inclusive of both male and female). And what would God's nature be? If we witness the power of nature, i.e. thunder, lightning, tempests, earthquakes etc. we might think such power manifestations are representative of a fearsome God. On our own, we cannot get a clear image of God, we need His help to visualize Him, to understand Him and His purposes. Has God provided this help to us? I believe He has. The operative word is *believe*. Just as we believe that a Civil War was fought in United States last century because of eye witnesses and recorded history, so too do we believe that God has revealed Himself through inspired writings. These writing we call Holy Scripture, of the Bible. we also have traditions and interpretations handed down to us from earliest times regarding the nature of a Supreme Being. Even so, nothing is clear cut, and all is open to discernment and interpretation.

The book of Genesis describes metaphorically the creation of the universe and the first man and woman. The author depicts a pastoral scene in the Garden of Eden where a serpent tempts the woman to disobey God. The woman does, and so does the man. This incident is known as the Fall and interpreted as Original Sin, thereby condemning humankind to alienation from God. A whole theology has been developed, whereby we are eternally damned unless we avail ourselves, receive from God his pardon through His

Son, Jesus Christ. It is our belief, our faith in Jesus that restores us to friendship with God, and hence our eternal salvation rather than damnation. This is redemption and atonement.

Traditionally, this process starts with baptism.

What is distressing with this interpretation is the seeming unfairness of guilt by association. I did not eat the apple! Just because way back when my first parents (and boy, that's stretching it) disobeyed God, why am I responsible? There is the argument that Adam and Eve could not pass on what they forfeited, i.e. friendship with God, and that all they could pass on was a damaged human nature, bent on sin.

There seems to be a complex, yet simple dualism in the nature of man. Not only is there a craving for God and goodness, there also is a tendency towards evil, defined as sexual abuses, injustice, hateful and hurtful actions towards other people, selfishness to the exclusion of others' needs, rudeness, lying, murder, drug abuse, war and on and on.

Some say this dualism is a result of *Original Sin*, and that human nature is damaged. Others say that human nature is okay, and that a person can choose how to act in a moral and upright manner without any external guidance. Still others take a middle course and say that we can do good deeds only by the influence of God by a gift of grace to enable us to overcome our sinful nature and perform virtuous deeds.

Dualism can be viewed as a condition of opposites. The first book of the Bible, Genesis, implies that in the beginning, God had a plan of contrasts or opposites. I don't believe we can understand the mind of God, but we can try to understand and discern what

our relationship to Him is. If everything was white, there could be no discernment because everything would be invisible, no contrast, all white, no visibility, much like a "White-out" in a snow storm. We can see marvelous contrast in all of nature. In our human nature, we see the dualism of good and evil. Evil is understood as a negative, a departure from God. All that flows from God is positive. Our first parents were all positive, there was no negative. The negative of evil and sin, i.e. turning away from God, was only possible in that it was part of God's original plan in that the highest faculty of God, if we can humanly speak of God's faculties, is His volition or choice: *He can do as He pleases, and has the power to do so.* When God created humankind, He chose to bestow choice. With this God given faculty, a human can elect to choose good or evil.

Another element that has been handed down by Scripture and tradition is the existence of a supernatural power that is known as the devil, or Satan. This is the prompter of evil and has as its mission, our destruction. I like to think of this power as Negative personified.

So, our God is a God of Risk, in that His highest form of creation can accept His dominion, companionship and love or reject it for that of another. Was negativity, opposition and contrast all part of God's original design and plan?

It seems that Adam introduced the negative into the universe through his choice of disobedience. Before that introduction, was Adam composed solely of atoms (no pun intended)? Was his basic structure like ours in the composition of protons (+) and electrons (-), or was the atom introduced through choice of disobedience, and passing on this composition of positive and negative particles that can decompose and die? If death, the supreme negative, was

brought about by choice, was humankind's decision a part of the original plan of God? We cannot figure out God's mind, but in order for Him to reveal His nature as compassionate Father, He would have to have something to save us from, something to assist us with, some hurt to heal. If we identify sacrifice, forgiveness , aging as signs of love, would not God need our neediness in order to express love to his creatures?

So here we have a human being, dualistically composed both materially and spiritually. This person believes in God and by his/her nature wants union with oneself, each other and God in a peaceful oneness of love. A person desires to reach his potentiality, to be actualized and to be the best. Can one achieve actualization without help? It would appear not. Even in order to reach one's own earthly destiny in time, it is evident interdependence with others is essential. How could we build our own houses, feed and cloth ourselves without assistance? All the more so to have faith, to perform virtuous acts, to love, requires help from God. This help is freely given by God and is called *grace.*

Grace is God communicating His life to us as interpreted in the Scripture passage: "In him we live and move and have our being" (Acts 17:28).

Grace is the love of God being perfected in us. It is the power and wisdom that takes the reality of positive and negative entities and through a paradoxical process produces a *both/and* results in the actualization of good.

Life is simply receiving God's grace and respond by manifesting love everywhere with a thankful heart.

The Action of Grace

> "I will sprinkle clean water upon you to cleanse you from all your impurities, and from all your idols I will cleanse you. I will give you a new heart and place a new spirit within you, taking from your bodies your stony hearts and giving you natural hearts." (Ezekiel 36:25-26).

In searching for the truth, there is nothing like a good dose of the Bible. Our bodies are our tents that carry us in our journey through life. As we rake the bacon, pull the pork, masturbate using pornographic pictures (graven images, idols), we become one with the images through our imagination and commitment to lusting after an orifice into which we spill cum. As we look at the sticky webs of jizz between our fingers, on our stomach and legs, we feel relieved, but at the same time, guilty.

We are abusing our tent and we know it.

Spiritual thoughts are 10,000 miles away and we want to keep it that way, but deep down there's a nagging. As Francis Thompson in the *Hound of Heaven*, put it so compellingly:

"With unhurried chase and unperturbed pace, deliberate speed, majestic instancy, they beat- and a Voice beat more instant than the Feet-'All things betray thee, who betrayest Me.'"

The love of God begins its invasion, not like an army but like a gently breath of air. The Holy Spirit, the love personified between Father and Son, floats like the feather in *Forrest Gump*, if we try to grab it, the feather moves away beyond reach. If we let it descend, it lands gently in our palm. The Spirit can be like a gentle zephyr or a mighty, raging wind. It can be a purifying cleansing stream, crystal clear, cool to the touch and gently washing our tents whiter than snow. The breath and power of God ignites our soul, fires our intellect so that we can now see clearly. We thirst for this Spirit of true love. We allow her entrance. We come to know her better through reflection on her stories in the Bible, especially *The Book of Wisdom, Proverbs, Ecclesiates and the Psalms.*

True love helps me correct my living a lie. I respect my tent, and the tent of others. I perceive that wacking off on a picture of a blown up twat, bent over rear are indeed very pleasurable and will probably remain so until my dick falls off, but realize its a lie and not in my best interests, or in the interests of my fellow pilgrims in this journey of life. Masturbation, cuts me off, isolates me, makes my heart grow as hard as my dick.

This hard, throbbing dick is a tool for satisfying a loving cunt. Typically, we are married to the cunt, but the woman we are married to is not just a life support system for a cunt, and neither am I a life support system for a dick!

There's more to life than jacking off. The Spirit calms me and helps me realize the truth, the truth of love. And then she penetrates me like no man ever could and plants her seeds of wisdom that bear the fruit of patience, courage, kindness, love and joy. She brings with her, temperance, prudence, self-control and harmony. We have the courage to change.

Gays, Aids and Structures

<u>G</u>ot <u>A</u>ids <u>Y</u>et? Not a very nice acronym, but like all acronyms, there's a ring of truth to it. The AIDS virus is carried in the blood and other fluids and in the male sperm. So, if another person ingests infected sperm, there you have it, AIDS transmission efficient and effective. Effective for what? Effective for death, dear heart.

Oh, there are a lot of non-gay AIDS victims, and these folks really got a bad rap. Some people consider AIDS as the avenging angel sent by God to get the gays. I don't think so. Some cheer it as a way to reduce the black population,. I don't buy than one either. It's literally a damn fucking virus that I hope goes the way of polio and we get rid of the menace.

I would like to use a comparison, however, between the pathology of AIDS and the pathology of sin. Both are a disease of the body and the spirit. The wandering HIV+ cell searchs for a victim white cell. Having found the victim, the HIV+ locks on, penetrates and injects the virus which changes the DNA structure of the white cell, destroys it and thereby weakens the immune system. Having *exploited* the victim, the reproduced cell goes in search of other victims, with the end result of death from the body's lack of a responsive immune system to ward off other diseases, such as pneumonia.

Sin, understood as a state of unbelief, in which this state enters the victim's innermost core of being, his or her intellect, will and

spirit. The result of this copulation parallels the invasion of the white cell, as the virus of sin yields a change of desire and behavior that produces evil actions. These actions go forth and hurt other people. Even personal sin becomes relational. Sin hurts not only the sinner, but the real malice is its evil effect on other people and the whole universe.

I'm not condemning the sinner, or the AIDS victim, but I am drawing a comparison to the activity of a dreaded disease to the activity of sin. Both exploit and are deadly to life.

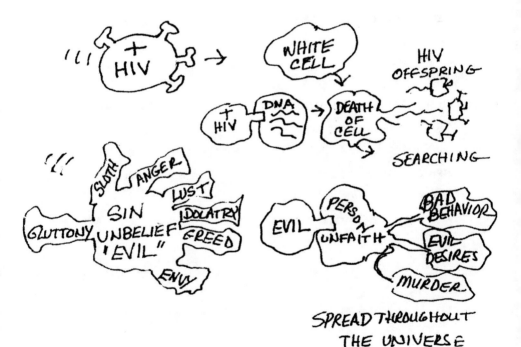

The Orgasmic Bible

Probably never thought of getting off on the Bible. It's true that a self induced orgasm can be ecstasy, it is also true that Spiritual penetration can create ecstasy without guilt. Listen to Paul:

"The word of God is alive and active, sharper than any double-edged sword. It cuts all the way through, to where soul and spirit meet, to where joints and marrow come together. It judges the desires and thoughts of man's heart"(Hebrews 4:12).

Reading the same passages over and over creates new thoughts and insights about God, myself, others and my dick. It's not a head trip (and here I don't mean head, like in giving head), but a journey of the heart. It's not the ability to spout quotations or give learned view or commentaries. It's not even the boast of reading the Bible from cover to cover. Rather the Bible is a prayer book of faith and love, where the Spirit enters us.

Slavery or Liberation?

"No, no, no, you've got it wrong! The term is 'self-love', not 'self-abuse'. Self-abuse is an old outdated term for masturbation used by some sort of fundamentalists or Catholics." As spoken by my sex therapist.

This sex therapist who I spoke with, may have a point. He thinks that masturbation is healthy and has no guilt association because it's merely fantasy. So, the question that is posed: is masturbation both good and bad, or is it either good or bad.?

Fundamentalists, quoting the incident of Onan in the book of Genesis, chapter 38, where he "spills his seed on the ground" and Catholics referring to Thomas Aquinas who thought that the seed contained complete human beings and therefore very sacred, both think that masturbation is gravely evil.

My thinking is that masturbation is fun. But sometimes fun can be dangerous. A single act of jacking off, not as a habit, or as a function similar in value to taking a crap, can be integrated into a healthy perspective. But the danger lies in masturbation becoming habit knit. For example, take smoking. I'm just kidding myself if I buy a pack of cigarettes and say, I'll just smoke one. Or, just a couple a day. Phooey, I'm kidding myself. Nicotine says to my brain, "Yummmy good, do it again!" And I'm right back on it, smoking at least a pack a day and turning my lungs to cork.

That's an addiction, and every little wisp of smoke does its woeful deed in the tender little cells of my breathing apparatus. It's just no good. Smoking is not a "both/and" kind of thing, it's either quit (no smokes at all) or eventually walk around with an oxygen tank pulled after you as you feebly walk with tubes up your nose.

Not a lot of fun, and definitely bad for your golf game.

As stated before, my addiction to alcohol needed to be healed. I am a recovering alcoholic and find so much more energy and clear thinking. Thank you God for this grace of healing.

So anyway, daily beating off can be compared to the nasty, harmful habit of smoking. Look at an ashtray full of butts and ashes, and look at the cum on your hand after jacking off. In both instances you want to clean up. If you don't buy into this kind of thinking, it's okay, it's pretty shallow anyway, and I'm no expert, just wanted to get you thinking. Hey, if you read this book and give up smoking you'll save the price of the book in a couple of days. Also you may have nicer later years still being able to breath without assistance.

Either/or thinking about masturbation can cause odd results. After nine years in the seminary avoiding deliberate masturbation, I found that I was jacking off in my sleep.

After 19 years of a frigid marriage, I found I was jacking off in my sleep, or when wifey was out, I might get off on a copy of *Cosmopolitan*. Now that I'm single for 11 years, but in a very committed relationship with a lovely woman, yet living apart, I find that I no longer jack off in my sleep, but now and then, get some porn and play around with myself. Sometimes preferring gay porno with self-stimulation to regular sex.

I read something recently that said homosexual orientation can be due partially to lack of spermatogenesis, or lack of sperm production. Perhaps my vasectomy of 15 years ago has influenced sperm production, and has strengthened a proclivity towards homosexuality.

Actually though, burying my face in another man's crotch wouldn't smell so good. I just like to fantasize with porno, the actual real activity would scare me, what would I say? "Gosh, that's a nice dick. May I suck it for you?" And the idea of actually sticking my tongue down his throat, or around and in his asshole, choke, makes me gag.

You know, cunnilingus, or licking the cunt, is pretty neat and tastes good too. It's very sweet, like honey. I never tasted another man's cum, but tried my own just out of curiosity. It was very bland and taste a little like chalk.

Be Fun to be around —
The Pillar of Success

1. Don't complain
2. Don't criticize
3. Don't bad-mouth anybody.
4. Give a constructive suggestion at work.
5. Daily, read something in your field.
6. Daily, read something totally different from current interests
7. BE A FRIEND.

PART 3: ...ON THE ROAD AGAIN

Divorce and a Book of 25 Cancelled Chicks

Work continued to have ups and downs. The up was I landed a job with another major computer company. After busting a few sales records and sucking up to the VPs I was promoted way beyond my reach. As Easter Region Manager, I had control and responsibility for 9 sales offices from Boston to Atlanta. Big hairy deal.

I inherited 9 so-so reps. One of the guys asked for a transfer after I played tennis with him and mentioned that some of my best friends were Jewish. Another rep sailed his boat on the Cape and made funny little selling gestures in the Boston area: put him in the chute. That was the bulk of the job, going to neat places with the General Division Manager and his gay side kick and putting people in the chute.

Speaking of chutes, one fine evening in Arizona, at an upscale lodging, sweltering in the evening spa smelling desert flowers, the GM's sidekick, Ralph, decided to slide over next to me without his bathing suit. He elevated his buttocks so that a semi turgid penis broke the surface of the hot tub. He rolled toward me and offered his Johnson for me to suck if I wanted to go down on him. After no response from me, he thought I might like to see his chute and go for it. So he brought his crack on the level of my face and separated

his cheeks. The GM just laughed and said "Aw go ahead, Ralph has plenty to spare."

Seeing that I am probably bi-sexual, I should have had sex with Ralph. But, still I didn't and to this day have not had sex with a man.

With smoke and mirrors we made quota, but it wasn't enough. Ralph was offended and persuaded the GM to replace me. Pretty ghastly scene as the demotion took place in front of my few remaining reps and I was given the choice to exit, or remain as a rep.

Bad choice, I stayed. Although sales were good and I made some scratch, I definitely lost face with the company and especially with Pam. She like being the wife of a manager.

Things went south at a very boozy and "romantic" dinner in which, through"lacka" of extreme duration, I told her that **"She was nothing but an armor plated, ball cutting, man destroying machine!"**

Love ended.

We left in silence, she continue without me driving into the night in our XJ12 Jaguar and blew the head gasket at 140 mph. The damn car always overheated after that. I asked her if she burned her lips when she "blew" the gasket. She wasn't amused.

She thought I'd be better off living elsewhere. I agreed and although I thought marriage was a one time thingy, I decided to get with it and find somethin', somethin', somethin' soon.

I met a young blond at Harvey's and she bought me a Bud. That was nice, She and a couple of her adolescent, pimply faced friends went

to her apartment. Leslie was an artist and liked pot. I never tried it, so I stuffed some in my pipe and lit up. Hmmmm, not much effect. I did like Leslie thought and wanted to get in her pants.

We went on the motorcycle to the Smokies and camped. We shared a sleeping bag, but she told me no sex, maybe a little cuddling, but that's it. After a few hits of grass and some burbon we hit the sack. I dropped my brief and "cuddled" big time. She kept on her panties so the best I could do was rub my Johnson on her thigh and leave a nice warm trail of spunk.

I wasn't doing too well with the younger set so I decided to join the Atlanta Sky Club. I was hoping for some good downhill, both skiing and otherwise. Off to the Rockies and superb skiing. The Atlanta Club put us up with a condo on the slopes with 6 girls rooming with us...it was a large condo. Well, the girls were just charming and married, or somewhat in between. The really sexy one with eyes that said f,ck me took to one of the younger guys. Not surprising. The other gals were friendly but just wanted to ski and be waited on. This was OK, as the skiing was *tres* terrific and I was trying to keep one of my married guys to not screw one of the rather unattractive girls. I figured it best for both of them.

The ski trips were just really real. One of the local trips included a rather drunk, actually very drunk 20 something girl who felt neglected on the bus trip home. She proceeded to sit on my lap and grind away while deep throating me. She kept saying lets go to the back of the bus where there was a john (not a pun) and we could screw in there. Tsk, she fell asleep before we got to negotiate to the bus toilet.

After many false starts, to include a one-nighter with a real coyote girl, while her son watched TV in the next room, I finally met an attractive 30 something at one of the Ski club functions. We hit the bedroom first night and the only thing that was a little bit of a turn off was that she had hairy nipples! Oh well, just stay with the muff. Liz really liked biking and we did a lot of DUI's on the motorcycle. Screaming down I75 at endangering speed while I did a wallet check on my back pocket, she squeezed her thighs and started to get damp. What kinda ended this thingy was she couldn't cook, was expensive and gave me the scavies. That's not a misspelling of skivvies, it's an STD that resembles the crabs..ugg.

Finally, a soul mate comes into my life. A little southern belle that took a shine to me.

Along Comes Maria

I met Maria as she was watching the same tennis match as I was. She was sitting there on the grass with several of her girl friends, smoking Winstons and remarking: "Wish I had a nice guy to play with." Well, here he is, the tennis jock himself: Mr. Moe.

It was boy/girl friend at first blush, and soon to develop into a great relationship in which I was definitely on the receiving end. What have we that we have not received?

Maria catered to my every need, she cooks divinely, does laundry, likes biking, and we do swell on the tenny courts. I taught her golf and we explored many golf packages each holiday break. I had my place, she had her dwelling. We just got together, no strings attached whenever we wanted to be with each other. I soon noticed it was pretty much all of the time. No strings attached, but she was shinning her love light on me and I was receptive.

One summer I decided to take the big Kawasaki 1000KZ for a trip to the outer banks of North Carolina via the Blue Ridge Mountain trail and Skyline Drive. Mary wanted to go, so we packed up and scooted. Can you believe a lady biking with all she needed for 10 days packed in a saddle bag? Whadda woman!

Funny, as I was stretched out on the grass by the reflective pool facing the Washington monument, my last beer was sitting next to me. Maria accidentally knocked it over. She was so distraught that she poured out her last can of TAB in retribution. Arrrhhh, not necessary I said, but too late. Whadda woman!

We moseyed along Route 12 where I was looking for a motel, a cheap one, right on the water. The outer banks are very sparse and natural with few lodgings. But presto! Tan-O-Rama appeared and it was right on the beach, about 100 yards inland from the Atlantic It had a nice screened in porch and cost $30 a night. Next door was a great Crab restaurant, also right on and inexpensive. The trip terminated at Oracoke Island, another gift from God, as was the whole trip.

Changes, Back West Again and Then Some

The Odysseys

Enjoying my bachelor days with sweet Maria, but still was abit bruised by the divorce. My working world was falling apart again, so I decided it was time to take an extended voyage that could be marked by many changes of fortune. This would be an intellectual and spiritual wandering or quest whereby I hope to find direction and inspiration as what to do with the rest of my life.

My ex-wife did a lot of nice things for me and to me. It may be unfortunate that she split, however, things have really turned out for the better, for me anyway. One of the nice things she did was to buy me a Honda CX500 motorcycle for my 40th birthday. This was a rather innovative bike. It was a 500 cc engine displacement (45 cubic inches) and had reasonable horsepower. A practical maintenance free shaft-drive, water cooled motorcycle that was like its car namesake built like an anvil. It was just the perfect choice of a motorcycle for my first 10,000 mile month long odyssey.

Unlike the modern bikes of today, I had no luggage capacity except for a sissy bar to lash my belongings on. Bummer! Saddle bags would have been nice. Oh well, I placed my "rat skin" a piece of lamb wool on the saddle and lashed a nylon sports bag, sleeping

bad and tent to the sissy bar and off I went motoring on back roads to California was indeed a bit of daring do, especially in the rain.

Bikers say that if you start out in the rain, you're nuts, but if you encounter it, that's bikin'. I was sipping a beer outside of Dodge City waiting for it to clear, when a Harley guy and gal saddled up on a chopper and headed into the downpour. The blond in tight short shorts murmured "Like, this will cool us off."

Over some George Dickel burbon, some fellow bikers said I really should take the circuit around the Rockies from Denver via route 40 to Steamboat Springs and drop down to Durango via some incredible scenic back-roads. Best advice ever!

A little chilly at Purgatory CO at 12000 ft., matter of fact, I was so cold and wet I could hardly keep the bike upright. Stopped at the only motel, and check out the price, remember now, I'm on a $50 a day budget. Ouch, they wanted $45 a night minimum. I stood there, very wet, cold and sorrowful looking asking for anykind of a discount. Hey, thanks be to God, I got the suite for $30. Oh, heavenly, a steaming hot bath with the remainder of my George Dickel. Went to the bar and met a couple of cowboys, Scruffy and the Wrangler. We had burgers and talked about out alimony and ex-wives.

Out the door and heading to Durango. Stopped at the town and met James. We talked about love lost over Buds and Winstons. Poor fellow, rather broke up. I offered to speak to him about the Lord and he was receptive, actually, he wanted a closer relationship so I used the Baptist formula for accepting Christ as Lord and Savior. I've only done this twice since I was invited by the lovely

Maryann to such a relationship with the Lord years ago. It goes something like this:

"I admit that I am a sinner and that Christ died for me and by His precious Blood I am saved and my sins forgiven. From this day on, I accept Jesus as my Personal Savior and give Him the management of my life as Lord."

James, like myself, accepted Jesus as Lord and Savior and we are much happier than we were before this commitment and conversion.

I tossed the ciggies, as I was trying to quit. I journeyed into the desert and camped in the solitude of the Mohave. I learned a couple of things from my talk with James. Alcohol brings out the truth, real feeling. Also, he said relationships are like trying to grasp a feather. The harder you push it, the further it evades your grasp. Best to let it float gently towards you and land where it will. If it comes near, it was meant to be, if not, let it go its way to another.

I think this is like it is with a woman and a man. If the woman really loves you and shines her love-light on you, you can respond and accept and make the most of a real thing. If you are the one with the light trying to attract the woman, it may or may not work. My own experience ended up by my ex saying: "I'm going to be another man's woman." Hmmmm, not nice!

The Pacific Highway is awesome on a bike. I camped at Malibu overlooking the ocean...wow! I climbed a mountain in the early AM and as I climbed I would think I was at the top only to find another horizon. A family of deer greeted me as I paused. I sucked it up and conquered the summit. I took out my paper back Good News Bible and reflected as I prayed a psalm.

The next stop was at a friend's house in Portola Valley CA. Bob and Linzy built a ranch near Bill Hewlett's house on multo bucks acreage overlooking the Pacific. Bob like to race Alfa's and had a Maserati Bora for commuting to work. Linzy seemed a little pale and remote and Bob seemed preoccupied with making a fortune. Retired early after some drinks and a light meal.

I followed Bob to his work as a General Manager and VP of a growing computer peripheral company. His booming Bora with 275 true horsepower and top speed of 160 mph was a challenge to keep up.

After a tour of the facility, I headed for my ol' birthing grounds at Modesto CA. I traced my steps to my first home and birthplace of my first son and wept. So many great memories that are no longer relevant. Oh well, scouted up some ol' buddies and stayed at their cabin in Groveland CA. I stretched out on the porch in black bikini briefs and thought about some porn and jacking the Johnson. The camp store had <u>Hustler</u>, cigs, and Henry Weinhard's dark beer. I settled for the beer and a great steak. Wrote some postcards and watched a hugh 4-point buck just a few yards from the grill.

Masturbation fantasizes would haunt me the entire trip, as well as my entire life! As the preceding intermezzo illustrated, I just love porno in all its varieties and wish I didn't feel so guilty and immature in jacking off. **It's so closely linked to booze, my profound selfishness and desire for pleasure.**

After a pleasant renewal of friendships, some golf and good eating and drinking, I saddled up for the return trip back to Atlanta. Something happened that colored the next couple of years. While dining with a close friend and sipping 1981 Marietta wine, a

spiritual discussion took place wherein I mentioned a sort of desire to take up studies for the Roman Catholic Priesthood again. I was encourage to do so.

Priestly Desires

I returned to my digs in Atlanta and thought about another job and the possibility of the priesthood. I talked to the pastor at my church who said he would put me in touch with the Vocations Director. I was told that I must first get an Annulment from my marriage.

The Annulment process is long and arduous. First your case has to be accepted by a member of the Tribunal. This done, the plaintiff must document a lengthy history and offer witnesses for further testimony in writing. A psychologist is employed at some point to determine if the plaintiff was of sound mind at the time of the marriage etc. After about a year, the results came in and presto: divorce Catholic Italian style, or in other word a granted annulment which declares the marriage never happened. Such foolishness. Anyway, the coast was clear to proceed with priestly plans.

During this episode, I took on a pretty neat job with a small software firm. I also told my dearie Maria my celibate plans. She was saddened, but, like a good trooper, still offered bed and other amenities to such a jerk as I.

The next odyssey was a trip to be interviewed by the religious order I was applying for admittance. I journeyed to New England and met with a host of interviewers. They said they would let me know. Took a little side trip to Nova Scotia.

The second odyssey came in thirds.

- 1/3 of the time visiting and interviewing.
- 1/3 of the time riding in the rain, usually a cold rain
- 1/3 of the time biking and enjoying great roads and good weather. At the conclusion I figured the trip was mediocre at best.

My biking junkets were mainly 10 odysseys of various duration covering 40 states and 2 Canadian provinces. Also included are 14 trips to Daytonaaaaah Fl for Bike Weekenderbenders. Oh you rascal.

Daytona Bike Week

To quote a popular title <u>Zen and the Art of Motorcycle Maintenance,</u> I would like to share Daytonahhh, and the Art of Motorcycle Debauchery. I have made 15 trips to this orgy of sound, leather and basically fat people, with short legs and huge guts.

The first trip was in 1982, a solo flight to a two-bit motel, normally renting its dark and dreary cubicles for $25 a night. Daytona week brought in twice that with a 3 night minimum stay. Oh well! Most memorable occasion was sitting on a street close to the beach, cigar in hand and a 16 oz Bud in the other checking out the sights of bunzy teeny bobbers on Spring break and a mixture of Bikers, with sounds of open pipes from a variety of bikes, not just blathering Harleys. Times have change and twenty-five years later it's mostly expensive Hogs with a smattering of crotch rockets and practically no classic Brit bikes, Italian or otherwise. Oh Well !

Also missing is the impromptu street-bike drags. Anybody could challenge anybody to lay some rubber. The sheriffs blocked off a . street and we were free to go. Also missing were the ol' Harleys that you had to kick start. In the heart of idling the old girls would overheat and quit. It was fun watch the dudes, particularly from South Carolina, kick and kick, unmercifully recalcitrant hogs that just would not start unless rested.

Speaking of South Carolina gents and babes, I wandered into the Boot Hill Saloon with a pint of George Dickel ("good for your

pickle") in my back Levi pocket and introduced myself to some SC folks. The way it works is you offer a swig, bop your head and stamp you feet to the riotous music and give the impression you would like to dance with Linda. Linda was Jeter's wife and if you wanted an early exit from life, you could stare at this fine, lean, brunette with gorgeous gams clad in a leopard bikini with modified chaps.

Anyway, Jeter says, "Linda, dance with Glen". That's the way it works, and I didn't even have a Harley or talk like Lewis Grizzard (a great American Southern humorist who has since exited with a bad ticker).

Other notable experiences were a tire puncture on my bike with an ice pick by some punks. Changing a tire on a bike is a trip from hell, especially if you have to do it yourself with a screwdriver.

One neat event was a Bike Demolition in which half crazed (or more probably completely insane dudes) bikers used their bikes to crash into one another til only one running bike and partially cripple biker remained. The show culminated with a biker attempting to jump numerous cars and crashing into the last parked auto. The drunken mob raised a howl and started to beat and dismantle the offending auto with their bare hands. The finale was a jet engine that was ignited and completely consumed the offending auto in flames leaving only ash. Crash and burn really sums up past and present Daytona Bike Weeks.

PART 4: CHANGES, TRANSITIONS AND RADICAL RE-INVOLVEMENT

Back to the reality of earning a living and looking at venues other than the Roman Catholic priesthood.

You know, the ancient Church of some 2000 years has a lot of beauty, tradition and truths. Church as an institution should not be confused or identified with the Church that Jesus Christ had in mind. Jesus preached and taught in the Jewish synagogues and was not very well received. Rather he took his show on the road. He wrote nothing other than some markings in the sand when confronted by the Pharisees accusing a woman of adultery and wanting her stoned to death (John 8:3).

I have had nine years of Catholic Seminary training before Vatican II (1963-65). I have had the best of both worlds of conservative Catholicism and the liberating theology of Vatican II. I would now like to get to the hidden agenda of this unusual memoir which is to address the phenomena of male sexuality in aberration.

Quite clearly in the *intermezzo* portion you read a stream of consciousness of pornography. The magazines, pictorials, web pages, newsgroups mentioned either explicitly or implicitly had for their purpose to excite and titillate a male. I would like to address the almost irresistible male urge to "get off", drop a load, cum, spank the monkey, mash the hash, in other words: "beat off" that is masturbate. This urge,depending on the individual male's,

makeup, personality, biology and sexual development, is hightened by viewing pornography and reading sensational, sexually oriented literature to engage the imagination, produce a roaring hard-on and culminate in semen ejection and relief.

Now then, what of this phenomenon? Surely as a male reading this you are aware of your reptilian and animalistic desire to have sex. I use these images to connote sex as gential expression, getting off, without the scantiest element of love. It is pure lust...just plain getting off.

I won't get into the area of other involvement in sex play, I will just concentrate on masturbation using pornography.

There are just so many avenues of titillation: magazines, books, newsgroups, web-sites, chat rooms and so on and on. The question is, is joy stick manipulation harmless or otherwise. Is it good for the body, soul and spirit, or is it malignant and harmful?

I've talked about this issue obliquely and explicitly in the *intermezzo* section and would now like to summarize without moralizing. It would appear that sexual expression through genital manipulation in a solitary fashion, using visuals to excite the imagination is profoundly and intensely pleasurable. The question is: is all pleasure OK ? Some would say, "As long as it doesn't hurt anybody, it's OK." But why then do men tend to do this sort of thing in private, in the john or shower if the wife is round and about. Why do they express themselves in this way when the wife is gone out and they have all their little pleasurable toys, lubes, dildos etc.laid out on the bed, in front of the magazine or tube, ready for getting off? Why is it so secret?

What if your wife came home early and caught you with your briefs around your ankles and wacking off in front of boys copulating on the tube. Is the shame and guilt anything that matters? Well, perhaps so. Lust is not just a solitary pleasure but uses your sex for pleasure without relationship or concern for another. It is completely devoid of love, except for the love of getting off.

There are boundaries. I think one can easily see how daily, or even twice a day masturbation with pornography can harm a spousal relationship. As we grow older, it takes more time to get stimulated with our spouse and achieve a lasting erection and emission. Oh there are aids such as cock rings and *Viagra*. But essentially it's a hard road to hold, and the embarrassment of a limp dick, not able to penetrate or do much else is not worth the hassle, so the male reverts back to porno and less work. The question is, how does this effect a spousal relationship? What does a woman think of a man addicted to masturbation using pornography? Does she cheer him on?

Also there is a disturbing thought that this behavior encourages the producers of porno in all shapes and ages. Many victims of tender age fall into exhibitions that will hurt their minds for ages to come. Just as chastity and pure virtue adds to the beauty and truly of our life on earth, so to does lust rot whatever it touches.

One last thought in closing is the second law of thermodynamics in which the phenomenon of entropy is described as energy dissipating to randomness, lowness of activity and in contradistinction to energy which is used for enlightenment and pure purposes.

One of the best descriptions of animal lust, getting off and all that precedes the quest and follows its completion is described by Sean Joseph O'Reilly in his book: *How to Manage your DICK (Destructive Impulses with Cyber Kinetics).*

"Let's look at the Dog Analogy. Dogs like to bark, copulate, defecate, eat and urinate on their territory, and sometime fight with other dogs."

See how the following list looks familiar when observing male behavior that has allowed entropy to reign supremely:

- "Mounting any bitch (female dog) in heat is done without hesitation.
- Puppie? That is the bitch's problem.
- Barking loudly is always acceptable at any time.
- Mark your territory with urine or excrement but make sure that the other dogs know what is your territory. It doesn't matter if the territory has already been marked.
- Fighting other dogs is not big deal and is always an acceptable way to pass time. Fair play is never considered. After all, one has teeth, which are for biting- biting is biting.
- Fight along is good but fighting in a pack is even better. It is a lot more fun to have a frightened victim that everyone can sink their teeth into.
- Some untrained dogs will eat until thy are ready to burst.
- Hanging out is really the only way to spend time. There is nothing else to do.
- Licking your balls and sniffing backsides is an excellent way to pass the time.

Perhaps more of Mr. Moe's journey sketches could be of interest, but actually, I think he has done what he intended. His journey continues with his putting alcohol and masturbation with porno in the same box as his "not smoking, ever again." Oopsie, perhaps it is abit of moralizing, but Mr. Moe truly believers that:

LIFE IS BETTER WITHOUT:

TOBACCO,

ALCOHOL,

AND MASTURBATION WITH PORNO.

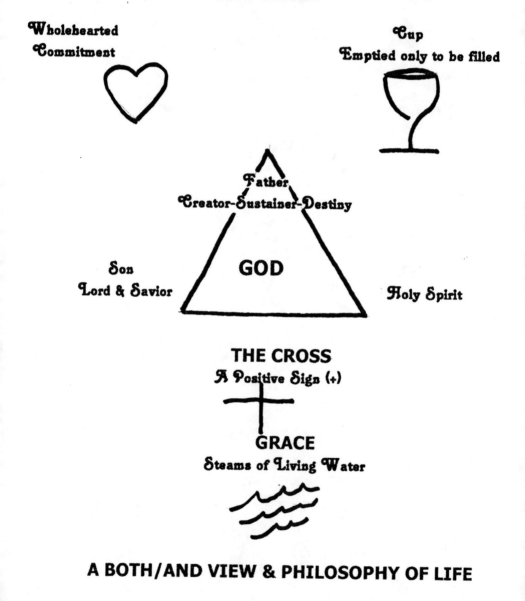

A BOTH/AND VIEW & PHILOSOPHY OF LIFE

POSTSCRIPT: WET

Please note than this section is a morality play and some parts are repeated from the preceding sections.

What is this feeling deep in the core of my being? A feeling of heat, desire a passion to express myself sexually. I want to build to orgasm, to explode in wetness.

What is this mystic desire for both union and transcendence? Is it a war between alienation and togetherness? Yes, all of the above.

I am complex. Truly a microcosm pattering the macrocosm of the universe.

I am alive and I both grow and die. A living paradox, a mystery.

I reflect. I must reflect, it is my nature.

"An unexamined life is not worth living." *Socrates*

A conscious stream of thought and conversation now ensues between the EGO: JOANNA and the ID: JOHN. Occasionally, the SUPEREGO: CHRIS will comment.

Cast of Characters

JOANNA. Reasonable, directing ordinary thoughts and processes needed for daily living.

JOHN. Instinctual, driven by passion, impulsive actions directed toward self- gratification.

CHRIS. Reflective, concerned with guidelines, norms and values.

CHRIS

All of another or us at one time have reflected on some aspect of our character and personality that displeases us. We call the aspect a fault. The fault can be further defined as an imperfection or even, for some, sin.

We all have faults. Most can isolate a particular fault as a predominant fault, that is, a real stinker that takes precedence over our other failings. For some it's pride, a real snootiness towards others expressed as: "You bake the bread, I'll eat it." Others may find the remaining six capital sins more to their liking/loathing: Greed, Lust, Envy, Anger, Laziness and Gluttony. They all have pride and rebellion as the core.

JOHN

My predominant fault is an obsession with masturbation and pornography. This obsession is the cornerstone for many other shortcomings: impatience with others, using other people in a manipulative fashion, intemperance in the use of alcohol and just mainly a mind-set of "what's in it for me?"

JOANNA

My assumption is that others are like **JOHN** in some degree, and are a little disquieted that they masturbate almost compulsively and prefer it to normal sexual activity. With vivid depiction and earthly language designed to catch the reader a little off center, **JOHN** seeks to pique the readers' interest. While **JOHN**'s narratives are titillating and appealing to the desire for pornographic imagery, with the help of **CHRIS**, I will subtly and sometimes not so subtly, offer reflections on the sacredness of the human person, relationships and the plan of the Creator.

JOHN

"Oh yeah, we all use to jerk off as kids. Sure, we all outgrew that stage as soon as we got our first piece of ass."

"I read *Playboy* and *Penthouse* for the articles. Once in a while I glance at *Men's Exercise*, not to look at the bulging bikini briefs, but to check out articles on fitness and health. *Cosmopolitan* and the Sunday paper lingerie ads are of passing interest, I would never think of taking them into the bathroom."

Of course not, we've outgrown such purulent interests when we got our first piece of ass in high school. Maybe some of us haven't outgrown this part of our sexuality. This is the story of **JOHN**, a seminarian for the Roman Catholic priesthood back in the 50's. The events are true, although, because some of them are embarrassing, names have been changed. The language is a little raw, but stay with it, we know that deep down you like to be talked to like this.

Boy, do I feel horny. Everybody is gone; I've got the place to myself and am completely alone. No kids, no wife, nothing until Tuesday

when they all come back. I look in the refrigerator and see the frozen lasagna she left. Not hungry, at least not now, I'm just horny. My last feeble attempt at getting some from wifey was met with little enthusiasm.... she made some comment that "is that all I think about? I'm more than just a hole for you to stick it in... etc." I'm going out.

Every time I go to the Union Newsstand, I feel a little sheepish. I hate to ogle at the used porno magazine section, but all the new stuff is covered with black plastic, no see through packaging. Use to be really good stuff I could get into, like XXX, now it's mostly soft porn like *Hustler*. Oh well, better than nothing. I'd like to look at the gay section, but all the other guys are checking out regular stuff, except for that one dude looking at *Blue Boy*. I think I'll just grab a cellophane pack of gay mags and another pack of girlie stuff and get out of here. The Chinese fellow at the cash register packs my purchases in a black plastic bag, just big enough to accommodate my delicious purchases. On the way out, a rather evil looking guy mumbles something like, "eat me." I'm not sure he said that, but that's what it sounded like.

Why did that sound so enticing? I remember a novel I read where the girl calls down from a tree to an irate neighbor "Eat me raw, mister." Sticks in my mind, as I hurry home to get something to stick in my hand. I can't wait; my dick is getting hard.

Home again, and a short stop by the refrigerator to fill a glass with ice. A generous portion of scotch follows and off to the bedroom. Oh, I forgot to mention, I'd given up smoking, but stopped by the Circle K to pick up a pack of Marlboros.

I need a few more things before I prop up the pillows and strip to my skivvies. First I place the dresser mirror so I can see between my legs when I'm on the bed. I really like to look at my swollen dick and bouncing balls when I'm gently stroking it while looking at some tantalizing cleavage, pulsating slits or bung holes. I saved a Gatorade bottle and have selected a carrot about the size of a young man's dick, not too small and not too large. A carrot to substitute for a butt plug or dildo, because I couldn't have such things laying around for the wife or kids to ask about. "Daddy, can I borrow your dildo?" No, I don't need that.

Almost ready, my dick is growing hard in anticipation. I take out a small jar of Vaseline and place it on the nightstand next to the little black bag. I remove my shirt, throw it on the floor, let my trousers drop, sit on the bed, pull of my socks, I had already kicked off my loafers. My dick feel semi-hard underneath my briefs, I give it a gently tug, it feels just great. I lay back, take a pull of scotch and light a cigarette. Oh boy, this is going to be great.

I take my first pack of books and tear away the cello packaging revealing an old issue of *Hustler*. I gingerly leaf through it and glance at the gorgeous cunts on display, I give my bone a gentle tug. The other girlie magazines are just as blatant, but the "girls" looked a little tough, sort of drugged, their eyes are messed up somehow.

I'm not sure I want to beat off just yet, and I feel an attraction towards looking at the gay male mags I purchased. The first one is *Rump*, and as soon as I crack the cover, I'm looking at a choice crack. A beautiful young ass with compact pink balls and cock dangling beneath a very desirable asshole. My dick goes ridged and pops out of my briefs.

I pull them off and throw them on the floor; admiring my swollen and lovely looking cock in the mirror. Why, it's just a big and thick as the boys in *Rump*. I stoke it and grab my balls. Hmmmm, feels so good. Much better than trying to pump my reluctant wife.

After we turn a few more pages, I fantasize sucking a fat swollen cock, and grab my penis pretending one of these Adonis is sucking me off as I put his cock in my mouth and lick it, suck it and wait for it to vibrate into orgasm, spouting man cream into my mouth and face. I'm just about ready to cum, but back off. I want to be fucked in the ass. I look intently on a large frontal view of a pulsating dick, and dip my cleverly designed carrot in the Vaseline. I slowly insert it in my rectum, every so gently. I'm surprised at how easily it goes in. Maybe I really could enjoy anal intercourse with a man. I shove it in about 6 or 7 inches, it feels so good. I can feel my sphincter close on the fantasy fuck, and unusual deeper muscles close on the make believe dick, or maybe it's my prostrate responding, something deep inside is happening and it feels great! I like looking in the mirror and seeing the carrot slide in and out.

Now I'm ready to fuck one of these pictures. Ah, here's a nice one, the young lad is bent over with his jock strap around his knees. He's spreading his buns inviting me to slip my head gently in his asshole. I put a little Vaseline around the rim of my Gatorade bottle. I held in under the hot water a little while ago and it's still warm. Oh yes, I had put my carrot in the microwave to give it a bit of warmth. Looking intently at the young backside entrance, I place the Gatorade bottle over my dick and thrust forward, imaging it to be the tight asshole I'm staring at. It is tight. I wonder if Gatorade made the neck on their products so much like a tight cunt or asshole on purpose? The warmth of the water treatment and the lube of the Vaseline do their job and I'm in.

I switch my fantasy back to getting blown, so I squeeze the bottle and it act just like I would imagine someone sucking on my dick. The pressure is very pleasing, and as I squeeze, my dick pops out. Well, all my senses are aroused, and I can't put it off any longer, I grab my dick and begin to pump it fiercely. Up and down, up and down, I look in the mirror; my balls are bouncing mightily. I glance at a particularly erotic picture I had selected beforehand that I would cum on, it's a picture of a young lad laying across the lap of another young man who is about to shove a dildo up his young chum's ass. Their balls are touching. Whoosh, out comes the man cream, lots of it, on my hand, my leg, the towel I placed under my butt. I think, "it doesn't get any better than this." I look at my hand and there are little strings of cum hanging between my fingers. I'm satisfied. It was great. I know I'll wake up in a few hours, turn on the light and do it all over again.

CHRIS
Nothing like getting off (ha) to a fast start. You weren't kidding about vivid description. But is this what life is all about? Isn't there something inside you that says "I feel a little guilty. "I've isolated myself from others and concentrated on sexual activity alone. It was pleasurable, but somehow I feel that it's wrong." Let's examine this feeling in light of where we come from, what we are and where we are going

The Truth of Existence, the real of Reality.. (This section has been copied from preceding pages for continuity of thought in Joanna's dialogue with John).

Before the dawn of time, there existed Existence. This existence always was and always will be, it is eternal, all-powerful the uncaused cause of all that has being.

How do we know this as fact? We don't. We are not made certain about the existence of this phenomenon we name *GOD* through empirical data. We have only the Bible (inspired revealed truths), tradition and our own intuition to guide us in our belief in God. Intuitively, there seems to be something inside of us that tells us that there is a God, and that this God is a Supreme Being who created the universe and us. By definition, creation means to make something out of nothing. Existence has to have a cause; it has to be brought into being. We postulate a pre-existing being to give being, and this is God. It is difficult to find a true atheist, one who denies God's existence. Rather we find agnostics, those who aren't sure, and we find those who would rather ignore God's existence and pursue their own agenda of independence and self-sufficiency. Even the atheist, in trying times or in moments of fear, will call out to a Supreme Being out of need. It seems to be part of human nature to desire God. Neediness seems to be genetic.

Let's examine human nature. We can observe our procreation in which in a marvelous manner, sperm and ovum are united and cellular division proceeds, bringing forth a human. just as all life on this planet, Earth, had to have an initial cause, the production of something form nothing, so too, there had to come into being the first man and woman. Because of our reflection on the nature of existence, we can postulate that the first man and woman were created by God. What kind of nature would God bestow? Would it reflect His nature? (I will refer to God as He, and use capital letters for clarity. It is understood that "He" is inclusive of both male and female). And what would God's nature be? If we witness the power of nature, i.e. thunder, lightning, tempests, earthquakes etc. we might think such power manifestations are representative of a fearsome God. On our own, we cannot get a clear image of

God; we need His help to visualize Him, to understand Him and His purposes. has God provided this help to us? I believe He has. The operative word is *believe*. Just as we believe that a Civil War was fought in United States last century because of eyewitnesses and recorded history, so too do we believe that God has revealed Himself through inspired writings. These writings we call Holy Scripture, of the Bible. we also have traditions and interpretations handed down to us from earliest times regarding the nature of a Supreme Being. Even so, nothing is clear-cut, and all is open to discernment and interpretation.

The book of Genesis describes metaphorically the creation of the universe and the first man and woman. The author depicts s a pastoral scene in the Garden of Eden where a serpent tempts the woman to disobey God. The woman does, and so does the man. This incident is known as the Fall and interpreted as Original Sin, thereby condemning humankind to alienation from God. A whole theology has been developed, whereby we are eternally damned unless we avail ourselves, receive from God his pardon through His Son, Jesus. It is our belief, our faith in Jesus that restores us to friendship with God, and hence our eternal salvation rather than damnation. Traditionally, this process starts with baptism.

What is distressing with this interpretation is the seeming unfairness of guilt by association. I did not eat the apple! Just because way back when my first parents (and boy, that's stretching it) disobeyed God, why am I responsible? There is the argument that Adam and Eve could not pass on what they forfeited, i.e. friendship with God, and that all they could pass on was a damaged human nature, bent on sin.

There seems to be a complex, yet simple dualism in the nature of man. Not only is there a craving for God and goodness, there also is a tendency towards evil, defined as sexual abuses, injustice, hateful and hurtful actions towards other people, selfishness to the exclusion of others' needs, rudeness, lying, murder, drug abuse, war and on and on.

Some say this dualism is a result of *Original Sin*, and that human nature is damaged. Others say that human nature is okay, and that a person can choose how to act in a moral and upright manner without any external guidance. Still others take a middle course and say that we can do good deeds only by the influence of God by a gift of grace to enable us to overcome our sinful nature and perform virtuous deeds.

Dualism can be viewed as a condition of opposites. The first book of the Bible, Genesis, implies that in the beginning, God had a plan of contrasts or opposites. I don't believe we can understand the mind of God, but we can try to understand and discern what our relationship to Him is. If everything was white, there could be no discernment because everything would be invisible, no contrast, all white, no visibility, much like a "White-out" in a snowstorm. We can see marvelous contrast in all of nature. In our human nature, we see the dualism of good and evil. Evil is understood as a negative, a departure from God. All that flows from God is positive. Our first parents were all positive, there was no negative. The negative of evil and sin, i.e. turning away from God, was only possible in that it was part of God's original plan in that the highest faculty of God, if we can humanly speak of God's faculties, is His volition or choice: *He can do as He pleases, and has the power to do so.* When God created humankind, He chose to bestow choice. With this God given faculty, a human can elect to choose good or evil.

Another element that has been handed down by Scripture and tradition is the existence of a supernatural power that is known as the devil, or Satan. This is the prompter of evil and has as its mission, our destruction. I like to think of this power as Negative personified.

So, our God is a God of Risk, in that His highest form of creation can accept His dominion, companionship and love or reject it for that of another. Were negativity, opposition and contrast all part of God's original design and plan. It seems that Adam introduced the negative into the universe through his choice of disobedience. Before that introduction, was Adam composed solely of atoms (no pun intended)? Was his basic structure like ours in the composition of protons (+) and electrons (-), or was the atom introduced through choice of disobedience, and passing on this composition of positive and negative particles that can decompose and die? If death, the supreme negative, was brought about by choice, was humankind's decisioning a part of the original plan of God? We cannot figure out God's mind, but in order for Him to reveal His nature as compassionate Father, He would have to have something to save us from, something to assist us with, some hurt to heal. If we identify sacrifice, forgiveness, aging as signs of love, would not God needs our neediness in order to express love to his creatures?

So here we have a human being, dualistically composed both materially and spiritually. This person believes in God and by his/her nature wants union with oneself, each other and God in a peaceful oneness of love. A person desires to reach his potentiality, to be actualized and to be the best. Can one achieve actualization without help? It would appear not. Even in order to reach one's own earthly destiny in time, it is evident interdependence with others is essential. How could we build our own houses, feed and

clothe ourselves without assistance? All the more so to have faith, to perform virtuous acts, to love, requires help from God. This help is freely given by God and is called *grace*. Grace is God communicating His life to us as interpreted in the Scripture passage: "In him we live and move and have our being"(Acts 17:28).

Grace is the love of God being perfected in us. It is the power and wisdom that takes the reality of positive and negative entities and through a paradoxical process produces a *both/and* results in the actualization of good.

JOHN
"Oh big fuck'n deal. While you were moralizing, I wrote a little poem for **JOANNA**, I hope she likes it."

ODE TO MY PENIS

 Glorious,
Standing so straight and tall,
I consider the wonder of it all.
At the center of my being
a fountain of life, penetrating the deepest secrets of
the universe in wet, warm envelopment.
To gusher forth a river of life
to be transformed with another, creating another,
a being, other than myself and mate, and yet partaker of
both.
The idea of course is intercourse for the ideal.

And yet, standing so erect and throbbing,
demanding release; balls full and fluid, blood hot and the hand
grasps, moves and jacks off to exquisite orgasm.
Oh wondrous part of my being and personality.
I thank God for making it so. I rejoice in my freedom.
Wet and wild, yet there is more than just being "a wet
end." "Eat me raw" is an enticement. Penetration a
form of slavery if that which is designed for release is
forced entered.
The pain of childbirth is not the same as the pain of anal
intercourse.
The imagination is not the reality. Truly, my penis is a love tool, a
tool of love for myself, others and the love of God.

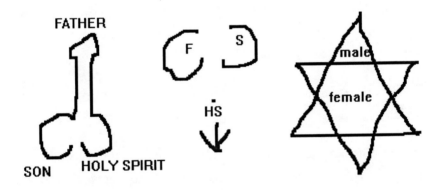

PHALLIC TRINDENTINE METAPHOR

The number seven (7) is a symbol for perfection. Many references in
Scripture use seven as a symbol for perfection. In the representation
above, the male genitalia is thought of as no. 1: penis as God the
Father, no.2 left scrotum as God the Son, and no.3 right scrotum
as God the Holy Spirit. The sex organ represents the Trinity. The
female genitalia also represents the female side of God: no.1 left

breast as God the Father, no.2 right breast as God the Son, no.3 vagina as God the Holy Spirit.

Merging together in the representation of the Star of David, a symbol of an earthy people, Israel, the triangles merge symbolizing intercourse of male and female, becoming one and yielding one

more through procreation. The **male** and **female** images taken together with divine significance and sharing in the power of creation yield 7: $3+3+1=7$

JOANNA
Really **JOHN**, that's a little much. Why don't we start from the beginning and tell me about yourself. Perhaps as I understand you better, I can make more sense out of what you are saying.

JOHN (Expansion and differing perspective from preceding pages)

I was a Roman Catholic seminarian for nine celibate years. My sex therapist tells me that I haven't begun to develop a normal sexuality. He tells me masturbation is just great and healthy. Get all the porn you can and flag that sucker. It's just fantasy, won't hurt anybody....good for you. Wellllll, I don't know about that, what do you think? Maybe I'm just another *guilty Catholic*.

Let's start at the ol' homestead, Schenectady, N.Y. back in 1943. My mother, now long gone, God rest her soul, was a beauty inside and out. She was from French-Canadian parents and met Dad while skating in Central Park. No, not the Big Apple Park, but the

lovely little pond in Schenectady. During the summer it was full of green algae and goldfish, with a spouting fountain. Come winter, it transforms itself into a mirror like glade that supports young and lusty blades, oh, spare me.

Mom was devote Roman Catholic and Dad a Lutheran. He was a good-looking Nordic rake, just in this country from Sweden for about six years. He picked up the lingo pretty well, as well as picking up my mom. He had these neatto racing skates, big long blades. I can just envision his blowing by Marie and radiating Swedish charm and deft moves. A real cut up.

Dad was on of the original CCC's, that's the conservation corps that built the Blue Ridge Parkway in the Smokies and numerous other projects that are much esteemed and beloved throughout the USA. He and mom headed out to Oregon to the Snake River to do CCC projects. What a glorious country, I still have pictures of that Eden. Mom was only eighteen, but a trooper. Dad showed her how to shoot a .22, which she need to do in order to keep the rattlesnakes at bay.

The firstborn died. Mom tried valiantly to keep her son alive, but he expired in the top drawer of a dresser, which was his bed. I don't know how a parent can overcome the grief of losing a son, but mom was a trooper and carried on. Her next son was playing in Oregon when a rattler was close to doing him in. Mom, a sharpshooter by now, but that sucker in the peep-sight and let fly a .22 piece of hot lead clean through the diamond shaped head.

Dad, now a Captain in the Army/Air Force, departed overseas to fight the enemy in New Guinea, an island just north of Australian and much prized by the warring Japanese Army.

Aside from dodging bullets and bombs, Dad related several unusual events. He was the "Old Man", the Commander of a group of about 500 men. In his quiet years, he was able to contact many of the lads under his command. They remembered, grouped together, celebrated and remembered some more. They cherished Dad; he must have been a really good Officer-in-Charge.

One day he was sitting in his office and a soldier came breathlessly in shouting, "Capt. Lawson, mad dog on the loose!" Dad chambered a round in his service Colt.45 and went out to see a snarling some-kind-of-mutt salivating and standing erect on a building foundation. Dad climbed up just in time to meet a full frontal charge. He calmly put a .45 slug between two fierce red eyes of the charging brute. No effect, the dog kept coming. He chased Dad around the foundation just like ring around the roses. Apparently the lead medicine finally took effect and Rover rolled over, dead.

Sure enough it was a clean hit, dead center in the dog's forehead, Dad was a great shot. Upon an inspection by the base doctor, it was discovered the dog's brain sat abnormally low in his skull, hence the bullet missed it completely.

Dad liked to shoot things besides the enemy. There were a variety of critters on the island; one in particular was the kangaroo rat. Dad would bag a few of these on the run and give them to a native, who would cook and eat them. Dad was a good ecologist, but had the misfortune of the native lad cooking his rats too close to Dad's paraffin treated tent. Whoosh, up in flames, along with a chest full of wartime souvenirs. I'll always wonder what was in the chest. About the only thing Dad brought home souvenir-wise that I remember was a green piece of tin like metal from a Jap Zero.

Dad returned home to Schenectady, and this brings us to 1943 and my first sexual stirrings. At the age of three, these stirrings can be summarized as looking up my grandmother's dress and a little incident with Janice. Janice was my playmate, because we lived on the same street, and rode tricycles. She was a year older, and quite mature. She led me behind my grandfather's work shed and offered to show her twat if I would drop my trousers. It seemed like a good ideal at the time, but somewhat unseemly, so I declined, being a young paragon of virtue. Many a night I wished I had looked.

JOANNA
"So even then, you knew that it would be wrong to do sexual things?"

JOHN
Yeah, even then it seemed wrong, but terribly exciting.

In 1945 when my Dad had returned form WWII, safe and sound. The next duty assignment was in Florence, SC. This was a lovely little sojourn of back woods southern exposure. Before we alighted in Florence, we had a short stay at Darlington SC. just beyond the railroad tracks in a rickety old flat owned by "Mother" McCabe. We just called her "Mother" She was handy with the ax, and could detach a chicken's head, pluck the little bugger, and have it ready for Sunday fare in a heartbeat.

In Florence, we went to school with no shoes, hung out and played with June Bugs. My romance was with a little gal next door whose mom use to cook us potato chips. I'm afraid my romance went as far as the chips.

Florence didn't last long; soon we were transferred to Hempstead, Long Island. Hot romance in Second grade. Her name was Barbara.

A lovely brunette who was hot. I'm now seven, still pre-pub, but an eye for the ladies. It must be my French-Canadian heritage, I always suspected my mom as being hot.

I peddled my bike to Barbara's home. One thing I really appreciated about my folks is the great trust and freedom they gave me in growing up. I could walk to town, or take my bike. If I wanted to, I could stroll over and sneak into the high school football games. It was just great. On to Barbara, she looked great, she was hot and wanted to do something physical, me too. She suggests "Spin-the-Bottle". She explained how it worked and produced the bottle. Round and round, it didn't matter where it stopped. We just smooched. It was great, but I was too young to get a hard-on, at least I don't remember one.

Dad got orders to go to Denver, Colorado. We bought a new 1949 Pontiac Chief. Cars were still scarce because of the WWII, and we were still clunking around in a 1941 Chevy. The new Pontiac was just a really cushy, big black road locomotive. The trip out west took five days, as Interstates were still years away and all the US routes went right through the heart of all the major cities along the way.

Dad would crack the nose draft and smoke Phillip Morris while taking an occasional sip of tepid coke. Bill, my older brother, and I sat in the front seat with me usually in the middle. Seniority has its privileges, including sitting by the window; once in a while we'd switch if I fussed enough. Mom sat in the back with little baby brother, Bob. Singing songs and being just a great, happy, Mom.

Denver back in the late 40's and early 1950's was paradise. The dry clean morning air, the lovely balmy afternoons were just downright the best place on earth. Bill and I use to cut lawns for $2. I'd get .50 for trimming. The remembrance of the aroma of that fresh cut grass in the Rocky Mountain air still sensually gratifies me.

My sexual stirrings had been on hold for a while. For the better part of Fifth and Sixth grade, I don't recall much of girls except for two, Rhonda and Beth. Rhonda was a big moose of a girl, much feared. She use to beat on me now and then. Beth had a round, attractive ass that I stared at and wished I could peek under her dress. Her ass got prettier when we graduated to Seventh grade at Smiley Jr. High. I'm now ten, and a truly happy pre-puberty child just beginning to experience the dawn of sexuality along with the dawn of religious experiences.

Her name was Pat Riley and she liked me. I know this because when I had chicken pox, she ventured to my home to visit and console me even though she risked very substantially, contracting this itching menace. I didn't care much for Pat, I rather preferred Margie Worley of the abundant breast. It was pretty much a challenge to "cop a feel" on Margie. We all talked about it but no one ever did. And then there was Jackie Orr, you can figure how we imagined Orr to mean, "whore"". We all talked about our expectations. We were all mostly talk, although some of us carried a "Trojan" in our billfold old, just in case. It was a badge of honor, even though it appeared used and wrinkly from much display.

My friend Gilbert was my first encounter with homosexuality. Gilbert use to like to wrestle kids to the ground and grab their privates. He would occasionally ask others to join the fun. I always felt a little violated by Gilbert so sometimes went along

with assaulting someone else in hope that I might avoid the same treatment.

There was this kid in Seventh grade named Mal. He was a latchkey kid, rather uncommon at this time. He use to like to flaunt his cigarettes and small vial of bourbon. There use to be for sale, a long cigarette that was individually packaged like a cigar. After he smoked the contents, Mal would fill these tubes up with bourbon and get a buzz on in school. One day during shop, he dropped his drawers in the supply room and started to beat off. Gilbert volunteered to help him.

My first masturbation occurred in the shower. I was soaping up and it just felt so good washing my dick. I kept rubbing it and then manipulated it up and down. It felt so good and suddenly I came. No one showed me, I didn't even know what it was. It's strange thought, how I went looking for a bottle to stick my dick in. Even then it was too large to stick in a soda bottle.

I had a friend, Ted, who seemed to be a man of the world. I showed him the "Trojan" I bought from Rob. Rob had several and always talked about getting laid. His most often repeated saying was "Jizz, the best nickel drink there is."

Ted didn't show me his dick. He tried on rubber, thought it was neat, rolled it back up and gave it back. It's a funny thing, but from time to time, I think of fucking Ted, or him sucking me off.

I had another Seventh grade latch key friend named Roger, who I occasionally fantasize doing mutual masturbation with. He invited me to his empty apartment after school one day and showed me his bathroom where he jacked off. He indicated he could sit on the tub and his the wall above the sink with a stream of cum. He sort

of indicated a contest between us, but still being the paragon of virtue, I decided to leave. Funny how Roger comes back into my middle aged mind. Wouldn't it be nice to go into an apartment with a young boy like that now and watch him jack off? Watch the expression on his face as he shoots his boy cum on the wall. Perhaps showing him a manly penis, much bigger and larger than his cock. Letting him touch it, maybe even letting him put the tip in his mouth to suck.

Life at home was serene. I would ride my bike home from school and mom would be there to greet me, ask about my school day, and them send me off to play after allowing me one Hershey with Almonds candy bar. Dad would whistle for me to come home for supper and my two brothers and I would join the folks for dinner. Mostly I picked at my food and had to be hollered at.

I was into a lot of hobbies and crafts, and if not playing baseball or other games with my friends, I would sit quietly and build models or draw and paint with watercolors. Just before bedtime, I would read "Donald Duck", drink Pepsi and listen to the radio.

Dad got orders to St. John's, Newfoundland. He went on ahead while the rest of us journeyed back to Schenectady to live with Grandma and pa until we could join Dad. I had a great time in Eighth grade. I had a little room in the attic and built models while snitching Camel cigarettes from Grandpa. I'd carefully blow the smoke out the window, hoping not to get caught. I didn't have any big deal sexual fantasies at the time, but was a regular in the bathroom after school jacking off. Grandpa suspected and even tried to open the door for a peek.

There was one girl in particular that had a reputation. I sat next to her in the movies and was trying to work up the courage to grab a feel. Never did, got plenty hot thinking about it though. She wasn't very good looking. The girl I really had the hots for was in the Ninth grade and my pal, Penmann, said she fucked for cigarettes.

Did I feel guilty about this as a kid? Sitting on the toilet seat, fondling myself until I had an erection, and then gliding my hand up and down my penis feeling the exquisite sensation until I ejaculated. Boy, did that ever feel good. But there was a sense of shame. I would flush the toilet so that if anyone were listening, they would think I went number two, instead of beating off.

CHRIS

Why the sense of shame? Genital excitation by means of using the hands for either the male or female is a normal tendency. Genital excitation to the point of orgasm is an extremely pleasurable sensation and sought after in many contexts. Visual titillation of pornography, video or just scantily clad individuals of either sex can start a process of masturbation.

The ethical and spiritual principle involved here is the self-focus on pleasure to the exclusion of others and possibly to the exclusion of God if the intention is sexual worship above all else. Preferring the created to the creator. In other words, the focus of lust to the exclusion of what may be right or wrong, pleasing or displeasing to God.

Scripture gives insight to the mind and heart of God, when it gives examples of men and women who have dedicated their bodies to sexual pleasures of impurity and have chosen these pleasures against the will of God.

The sexual urge is important in bringing the sexes together for love of each other and obeying the will of God in working with him in procreation. Like all passions, i.e. anger, guilt, fear and worry, the passion of lust must be controlled by wisdom, love, prudence, temperance, justice and the courage of the grace of God to make the effort. Unfortunately, the effort is difficult, and the yielding to the passion of lust very easy and tempting.

JOHN

You really do sound like some kind of prick. Next, you'll probably quote some authority that asks the question: "does masturbation accurately express the fact that a person's fundamental relationship with God and others is being intentionally curtailed?"

I had enough of this type of bad advice to make me sexually immature and confused even to this day.

JOANNA

You poor dear, perhaps you can continue and we'll see what influences helped shape your confusion.

JOHN

We joined Dad in Newfoundland. The four story wooden frame dwelling we rented on Ordinance St. was built like a chimney and would have burned ever so brightly in a few seconds should and errant cigarette enkindle it. We were on the top floor and would have been a burnt offering. I still continued masturbating, but began to feel guilty about it.

Church was an annoyance which my brother Bill always felt the need to comment how boring was Sunday mass. My mother always corrected him and reinforced the ideal of how good God is and has been to us, and that we should be grateful. Confession and Holy

Communion were relics of the past, and we attended Sunday mass dutifully, but with little participation. The reawakening of the need for confession was the experience of masturbation. I felt guilty, but didn't know why. It felt so good and all the kids did it.

What really hurt me was confessing masturbation. Father would ask if I "went all the way and produced seed." He them counseled not to do it anymore and to avoid the occasion of sin. I felt relieved, but troubled, especially when I would do it again.

Another really hurtful influence was a book called "Youth and Chastity" by Fr. Kelly. Here I was introduced to venereal forbidden pleasures of touch and thought. Here were ironclad proscriptions and restrictions with a whole bag of "no-nos".

The base chapel at Pepperill Air Force Base in St. John's was the typical military chapel; a single, simple room with pews and sanctuary. The sanctuary accommodated the three main religious faiths of Catholic, Protestant and Jewish. Behind the sanctuary was a small office and vesting room. Inside the church and to the right of the sanctuary was a confessional box.

Father Devore (Major, USAF), was a delightful, patient man who instructed me in the Latin responses and the ritual of being an altar boy. The love for the liturgy and the Mass interested me in buying a book explaining the Mass in beautiful prose with inspiring illustrations. My interest further developed and I purchased a daily missal, a beautiful volume, encased in leather and printed on fine, nice to feel, paper. I had it blessed by the Archbishop of St. John's basilica where I began to attend daily mass. The basilica was an ancient gothic twin spired magnificent structure that engulfed me in shadows, candles, incense and statues. The mystery of God and

his caring presence imbued me deeply. This is when I heard the call of a vocation to the priesthood..

JOANNA

So, I see a radical change-taking place here, from a normal child to teenage development there is a transcendent feature bringing you into the area of mystery and awe. What happened next?

JOHN

In the Fall of 1952, at the age of thirteen, I went to a High School Seminary in St. Nazianz, Wisconsin. My parents and Fr. Devore choose this seminary because it was located 90 miles north of Milwaukee, Wisconsin where I had relatives who could help out and look after me while my folks were in Newfoundland.

We packed a big steamer trunk full of clothing, linens and whatnots all carefully labeled with my number #302. Dad and I flew military transport to Westover Air Force Base in Massachusetts. It was a propeller two-engine job, with seats along the cabin wall facing cargo in the center. A bit chilly, but fun, especially the box lunch. Mom and Dad were great to let me go, the freedom they'd always given me still endured. My brother Ralph had left Newfoundland for college in Denver, and with me gone, it just left Mom with the baby, brother Bob.

Aunt Chris and Uncle Joe picked me up at the train station in Chicago. I sat in their 1949 Chrysler while they went into a downtown Chicago department store to do some quick shopping. Suddenly, somebody did a fender bender on Bob's car, hesitated for a minute, saw that it was just a kid in the car and drove off. I figured they weren't going to stop so I remembered their license

plate number. Uncle Joe was really appreciative and was able to get recompense later.

I was delivered to Salvatorian Seminary to begin studying for the Roman Catholic Priesthood. What a wondrous setting in 1500 acres of rolling northern Wisconsin hills, the gothic styled church and seminary buildings were serene and inviting, especially in September when the apple trees flourished close at hand. Early in the morning, I could reach under a heavily laden apple tree and pull a cold and still dew covered "snowball" variety. They were small, juicy and pure white on the inside.

The rule was pray when it's time to pray, play when it's time to play and study when it's time to study. The living was very compartmentalized. God became the center of my life and helped me make sense of all external things, happenings, events, joys and sorrows. The mighty theme of AMDG: *Ad Majorem Dei Gloriam* (all for the greater glory of God) was prevalent in all things: studies, prayers and play. The rule of the seminary was my rule; I lived and breathed it.

I think the seminary experience of compartmentalized living had both a positive and negative effect on me. I still compartmentalize and it enables me to focus and accomplish actions without interruption. In the broader context, my compartmentalization did not allow for a total giving of self to another in marriage. This may have been an extreme request, spoken and unspoken, on the part of my spouse; this demand for exclusivity of affection and attention when solicited. Compartmentalization led me to give quality time to my spouse, but not all my time. I did as I pleased, and pleasing me did not like an undue amount of sacrifice. Sacrifice demanded by "honey-do's (Honey, do this, do that etc.). However, like most

husbands and fathers, I did compromise and found delight in some tasks, and in others, distaste. I think eventually compatibility could have been worked out, but unfortunately the tension resulted in perceived "irreconcilable differences" with the usual consequence of a broken marriage, and broken heart.

I didn't have much trouble with "no girls" and the idea of the irrevocable vow of celibacy during the 9th and 10th grades. When I became a Junior, I began experiencing nightly hard-ons with accompanying erotic images. As I drifted off to sleep, I would begin to rub myself against the mattress, or unintentionally fondle myself. Frequently I would ejaculate.

This was matter for the confessional, but as I was only half-awake, there was little if any culpability. As a matter of fact, by the time Senior year came about, I was rather enjoying the event, and was glad there was no sin attached to it because I wasn't able to give full consent of the will due to my semi-conscious state.

Almost unbelievably, I remained "pure", no intentional masturbation for the entire nine years of seminary life. This also included summer vacations. Nightly occurrences were frequent and sometimes a little questionable as to how awake I was.

Throughout my nine years in the seminary, 1952-1961, I never encountered a queer, or a faggot priest. My own sexuality was comatose, however there was a kid who had a really nice round ass which I somewhat admired. If I felt a sexual stirring I would immediately practice custody of the eyes and look away. I had the same stirrings in the locker room where boys put on jock straps. There was one guy name Phil. He was an Italian stud with a huge

ball sack. His dick was very thick, but short. He left the seminary in a couple of years attendance and married a very fertile girl. They had lots of kids.

What finally happened, was the Disciplinarian at the major seminary counseled me to leave, as he thought this nocturnal habit might cause me some problems later on, and that perhaps I wasn't suited for a life of celibacy.

JOANNA

I'd like to discuss two things with you before going on. First the development of a masturbation obsession and secondly, your broken marriage.

So you found yourself at night, playing with your penis. Did you have sexual fantasies while you were fondling yourself?

JOHN

Well yes, but it was in a semi-conscious state, so I wasn't guilty of impure thoughts. And since I couldn't give full consent of the will, there was no sin. As a matter of fact, I began to enjoy it and look forward to it. These fantasies weren't homosexual at the time; rather it was a kind of misty imagining of a girl/woman. You know, I didn't even know what a cunt looked like. I remember asking my spiritual director if we would be able to see pictures of a vagina so we would know what it looked like.

JOANNA

This sounds like the worst kind of counseling as well as a seeding ground for sexual neurosis and obsession. The spiritual director

gave you good advice regarding celibacy. You needed to have someone help you adjust and mature in a normal way.

About your marriage, tell me about it, what went wrong?

JOHN

A little background first. I was home from the seminary, home for good. It was around Christmas time, and I had made the decision in 1960, at the age of 22 to begin a new life. Nobody was home at my parents' house and I felt like a drink. My first real drink. I called the liquor store and asked if they delivered, not having any wheels at the time. I also asked what might be a good whiskey that was affordable. The guy on the other end of the line was a nice guy, patient and helpful. He said that "Ten High" by Hiram Walker was a good four-year-old bourbon, sour mash and $3.95 delivered. A done deal! I poured one shot glass 1/2 full and savored the dark brown, deliciously scented booze. It warmed me immediately and I felt a little nervous, as I didn't want to be sick. You see, at the age of 19, I went to a seminarian party here in Schenectady, where the partygoers were all regular high school graduates, just newly entered into the seminary. They could hold their beer. For me it was new experience, and I got totaled on 2 beers. Boy, was I sick and I had to sleep over. The boys tried to help me walk it off, but to no avail. They called my folks to tell them that I was zonked out and would be home in the morning. I didn't want to get sick again.

I don't ever remember finishing that bottle of "Ten High", or even what happened to the bottle. Drinking was not a priority, and I seldom drank unless I was partying. We had a neat group of guys and gals at the CYO (Catholic Youth Organization), and this outfit put together a "Dude Ranch" weekender bender. Marie came with

me and was she hot. A nice little Italian girl that just loved to smooch and make out. Of course, being just out of the seminary and still a celibate (yes, a virgin at 22), I was still in the kissy-face stage of my sexual development, hadn't even copped a feel. Well, a quart of Ballentine scotch, yes, they still had quarts, not 750ml, or liters, but good old solid quarts of booze, accompanied Marie and I to the dude ranch. We arrived Friday evening and immediately started square dancing. I poured a generous scotch on the rocks and off we went. After working up a pretty good sweat, (when you're young and celibate, sweating is OK, you don't seem to smell badly) Marie and I disappeared under a nearby pine tree with our bottle of Ballentine. We rolled around in the grass, hugged and kissed, nice long juicy kisses, but I still didn't venture a hand up here dress. I didn't feel her up, that would come later.

My first sexual encounter was Saturday in Marie's room. We were lying on her bed, fully clothed, smooching away. I unsnapped her jeans and slid my hand down her very small and virginal crotch and let my finger do the walking. I put one finger in her vagina and slowly finger fucked her. I enjoyed this immensely, never having felt a cunt before. I put in another finger, boy, was she ever tight. We did this for probably a couple of hours, she never touched me and I had a rod that could have supported the World Trade Center. But you know, I really wasn't focused on myself, my attention was entirely on Marie and her lovely lips, both above and below.

I felt guilty, and because it was Saturday, sought out a church with a confessional open for business. As luck would have it, there was a small Catholic Church nearby and I unloaded my guilt ridden soul. I promised to avoid "the occasion of sin" and try again to be pure. Marie hung out with her girl friends and I avoid her. She must have felt a little guilty too, as she was standoffish. Well,

St. **JOHN** (that's me) finished the weekend and we jumped into our friend's car, Marie and I in the back seat along with several others and headed back home to Schenectady. Marie and I in the back seat became re-acquainted with long, luscious kisses. That girl truly taught me how to kiss!

That summer I went to Newport RI as an officer candidate for the US Navy. Marie wrote me daily, little cute cards, passionate love letters of desire. She was one hot chick, and helped me, the former seminarian, get through a tough military course of which I knew zilch. I would even put my spats on backwards for marching drill and hurt my hand doing gun maneuvers with an M1 WWII heavy-duty rifle. But Ah, there was an interlude.

Marie and her friend Maureen, were able to con Marie's mother into letting them drive their 1952 faded green Dodge to New York city. I had a friend, Arnold, who lived in the city and gave me a weekend lift to meet Marie. It was wonderful. I was dressed in my Navy blue midshipman uniform, complete with snazzy white combination cap. The girls really go for a dude in uniform, especially a 6'2" slender virginal dude. We walked and talked, toured NY, took the Staten Island ferry for 15 cents each. A lovely, inexpensive diner of spaghetti at a sidewalk Manhattan outdoor cafe set the mood bedtime.

Marie and I chastely slipped under the covers with our underwear on. We were quiet, as Maureen was in the bed next to us, probably pretending to be asleep, but more than likely being all ears. We kissed and she led my stick prick to the lips of her very small cunt. I couldn't penetrate. It was like trying to stick it in a coke bottle, just wouldn't fit. I literally popped out, not having gotten past the first set of lips. Oh well, I thought it was God's will and besides, I

didn't have a rubber and never have fucked anybody anyway. So I left NY with my virginity in tact, but an older and wiser man. My dick did eventually go down before I returned to base.

Marie and I never made it to the altar. I graduated from OCS (Officer Candidate School), Newport RI and was mighty proud. While I was home on leave I strutted over to my old working place where Marie and I use to send each other loves all day long and cut out at lunch time to smooch. I was really showing off in my natty midnight blue uniform with the gold braid of Ensign on the sleeves. My white combination cap with the Navy Seal was just too stunning. I was surprised I could get away from the mirror at home long enough to make the fashion show at the Bureau of Tax and Finance. This was an hourly job that I had before joining the Navy. It consisted of rows and rows of keypunch machines where we processed tax returns. I was one of three men amongst 500 cunts. I had an especially nice cunt as a supervisor. Her name was Rose and she let me get away with murder. I was a lousy keypunch operator.

Marie and I were engaged but trouble was brewing. You see, her Italian Mom wanted to invite all of Italy and Sicily to the wedding. OK by me, but Mrs. Whop thought that my parents should pay half the bill. My folks said they consulted a book from the library that indicated their responsibility ended with the boutonnieres for the ushers. The "consulting a book thing" drove Mrs. Whop bonkers, and henceforth there was a serious Italian plot for nailing my knees to the floor.

The whole thing blew at the bowling ally. My good friend and male chauvinist Tom and I took the girls bowling. Tom was a

body builder and use to like to take girls to his apartment while he worked out in spandex briefs.

The girls mainly threw gutter balls and after a considerable patient endurance of their bowling ineptitude, Tom and I cordially ask them to sit their asses down while we bowl *mano a mano*. The girls were incensed and squawked big time, but to no avail.

The next day, my mother got a call from Marie and was informed that Marie was never going to speak to me again, ever. The wedding was off and she would return the ring after I departed for my ship. End of story, except the following Christmas I got a card from her mother requesting that I send back a watch she had bought for my graduation at OCS.

Well, here I am in the Navy and still a virgin. We cruised down to Santa Domingo, a little town located on the Caribbean island of Haiti. We steam into port and we officers, nattily dressed in our white shorts, matching shirts and sock and white bucks head for the watering holes. I met the nicest girl, and she took a real interest in me. She led me up the stairs and I put a deposit of $2 on a little room and a towel. I began to get the picture when she snaps off what little she had on and begins to blow me. I almost came immediately, but decided I wanted to try my first ever fuck. So on her back she goes and I enter her. Gangbusters, it's so wet and warm, I just love it. She starts pumping mightily and I slow to relish the whole sensation. She takes the pause as meaning that I came, but in fact, I hadn't. She jumps off and heads for the **JOHN**. I hear a toilet flush and she's back with her panties on looking for money, she wanted $5. To my embarrassment all I had was a cheap pocketknife, a 1/2 pack of Luckies and $2.80. She took it all and went back downstairs.

Back on board ship I told my friend Jack that I was a little worried that I'd catch something. He laughed and said if I don't start dripping, don't worry about it.

Back in the states we use to go to the Little Creek Officer's Club and get sloshed. We had absolutely nothing working for us and couldn't fine any chicks. One night we were nursing our pitcher of beer when the asshole Marines sitting at the next table began singing offensive songs. We offended right back by throwing what was left of our pitcher of beer on the Corps. Tables flew, and so did I, right across the floor into the jukebox. Their leader looked like Frankenstein and was about as big. I could see a massacre coming so I stepped up to Franky and said: "Whoa Dude, let's be gentlemen about this. Choose a weapon and let's step outside." He replied: "Knives," and produced a rather evil looking pocketknife. I headed out the door and he was following after me. Fortunately, my 1963 VW was close at hand, I hopped in, turned the headlights in his face and yelled: "I choose Volkswagens", and headed straight for Franky. He jumped out of the way and I headed back to the safety of my ship.

We had a lot of deadheads on board. I once cracked the code on getting some nurses on board for a movie. They were cute Norfolk student nurses and it could have been the start of a supply of twat. I brought them into the wardroom and my fellow dick-head officers didn't even get off their asses to greet them. Matter of fact they ignored them during the whole flick. I tried to get some of my buddies to get with the program and join us in taking the girls to the "O" Club. Snore, gotta go, got the watch, yawn etc. They all departed and left me with the girls. I apologized for my seemingly gay wardroom and took the girls to the Officer's Club. They were

instantly snatched up upon entering by Navy aviators and I never saw them again.

I talked to the XO, (Executive Officer) of our ship and asked if he could do anything for me in the way of getting to Washington, DC as a duty station. I had paid a couple of visits there and the girls outnumbered the guys 8:1. He came back and said a detailer friend of his could line me up with a billet in the Office of Naval Intelligence, but that it would be career suicide for a young Naval Officer to request shore duty so early in his career. Fuckin'A man, suicide-city here I come.

Before departing for DC, we had a Mediterranean Cruise scheduled. I could either go and be detached overseas, or go directly to my new duty station in DC. I told the Captain of our ship, I couldn't afford vacationing in Europe, to which he responded, he'd go into debt for a year to make such a trip.

Doug, a fellow officer who also was changing duty stations, decided to make the trip with me. We were detached in Naples, Italy, and immediately secured a red VW for our search and destroy mission of hunting foreign pussy. First stop was at the Allied Officer's Club where we loaded the back seat full of booze for about $20. In between our seats sat a huge jug of Italian Red wine for constant consumption as we motored north towards Rome. We met some twat at the leaning Tower of Pisa. Not especially good looking girls, but they could speak English and were girls. After they related a story how they were picked up by some uncouth Italians and managed to get out of their car by stabbing one of them, we decided that any sexual advances on our part might not be welcomed.

After fruitless missions, we finally encountered two beauties sipping warm beer on the Champs Elysees. We invited Ruth and Zelda to the Follies Bergere and picked them up later that evening. The plan was to get laid as soon as possible, but as it turned out, we just really enjoyed their company. We went picnicking the next day and toured Paris. It was going to be our last night so I figured now is the time. Well, Zelda didn't want to, she said she was Catholic and was saving herself for marriage. She also said she had fallen in love with me and maybe she could come to the States to visit. I think she had some pretty good coins as her Dad own some resort in the Black Forest. She was a beautiful tall girl with long black hair and flashing green eyes. She did write several letters and even sent pressed flowers in the letters. So very sweet, but I wasn't ready for marriage yet.

Doug and I boarded a plane, one with propellers on it, and flew across the ocean to our new duty stations. My new assignment took me to the Pentagon in Washington, DC. I was really lucky to find a pad to share in DC. Rents were high and my income of $278/month, low. What a crew: a Seismologist, a Chemist, an Oceanographer, an Economist, a Civil Engineer and yours truly, a LTJG in the US Navy, made up our household. We kicked off my initiation and welcoming by a blow out party. Since the ration of girls to boys was so heavily in our favor, we just carried invitations to our party with us and gave them to all the good looking females we saw. We didn't worry about the guys as they all found out about it through the great DC grapevine. Dressed in our vests to identify us as hosts, we set out numerous kegs of beer. We had a guest book for signing in and after the party we would as a group evaluate the chicks and make comments in the margin. Obviously there was a

place in the book for phone numbers, and behold, a prospect list comes into being.

I remember this one girl in a short tennis skirt. After she passed out on the couch removed her panties and looked at the most beautiful little twat I'd ever seen. Of course I hadn't seen any to date, all the snatch I've previously encountered was in the dark. But this little peach of a cunt was exposed in the stark light of a lamp by the couch, it's fine amber hair adding a nice perimeter and frame to a lovely smelling slit. I got a real boner, but recovered from my alcoholic impropriety, pulled her panties back up and started to behave myself once again.

I did have one successful sexual experience that I didn't have to pay for early on in DC. Laura was a friend of a friend, so she trusted me. She was hot and definitely wanted to screw. I stopped by the drugstore on the way to the beach and picked up some rubbers. I was so cool as I said, "Excuse me while I pick up some blades." Is that cool or what?

It was dark when we got to the beach, which was pretty close to her home. I spread a blanket and after some feigned amorous kisses, grabbed her twat and started rubbing. In a heartbeat, I had my trousers at half-mast and unrolled a Trojan (non-lubricated) over my swollen young dick. I began to jam it in. It was a little difficult because of the sand, her not-yet-wetness and my inexperience. I came fast. I don't think she thought it was too great, mainly because of the sand in her crack.

I slept in the guest bedroom and wanted to invite her to join me for another round of fucking. The problem was her mother. She had the bedroom next to her daughter.

The next day we went for a ride and ended up at her Dad's in-town apartment. Dad wasn't there so we proceeded to the bedroom. She was wearing pee-yellow panties, which kind of turned me off. Oh well, on with the rubber and a quick lay. She seemed to enjoy this a bit more and starting mentioning the "L" (Love) word. Opps, time to race. She wondered if that was it and if she'd ever see me again. I assured her she was just a recreational fuck and that was it. Good-bye and good luck.

I was still trying to develop some sort of sexuality. I was still restraining from masturbation and had not the slightest of homosexual tendencies. Asking my buddy **CHRIS** to help out, let me just share some of my more moralistic thoughts about homosexuality that were my thinking at this time.

CHRIS

Consider a sexual metaphor of two becoming one through sexual intercourse. Each person retains their own identity, but during the act of sexual intercourse, the penetration of another human being by a sexual organ occurs, and at the moment of orgasm, fluids are exchanged.

Aside from the intention of the people coupling, which could be a true love for one another and a desire to become one through intercourse, or the intention could be selfish love and merely a desire to find release of passion, there is nevertheless a unity of fluids.

In the former case, i.e. the unity of true love, the sexual act may be open to the transmission of sperm to the fluids of the vagina and carried to the ovum where penetration may occur once again and the two truly become one in the conception of life and a potential

190

human being, a child. In the latter case, consummate lust could also produce the same results, and the child paradoxically is sometimes referred to as a "love child."

To think in terms of natural and unnatural acts, we analyze what "Mother Nature" has in mind regarding the naturalness or nature of the sexual act, in other words, *what's it all about?* To what purpose is the sexual act for? Does it have meaning and purpose, or is it akin to blowing one's nose, and the resultant fluid mass having equal value, or non-value?

If we think Mother Nature as a myth without meaning, we can translate this to an unreflected life and that meaning is only personal. There is no meaning except subjective meaning, that which pleases me is the only important consideration. Masturbation is a good example of divorcing meaning from sexuality. There is not joining of fluids for the production of anything, merely the release of ejaculatory fluids into the hand, or elsewhere.

Mother Nature is, of course, a personification of nature. In the Christian-Judaic culture, nature does not stand uncreated and alone; rather it is the result of creation and a Creator (Creatoress). Christian tradition has passed on the image of Christ and his Church as bride and bridegroom. The metaphor suggests the meaning of sex as a foreshadowing of the eventuality for the unification of all creation into oneness, the harmonization of all positive and negative elements into the peace and serenity of love..

As far as same-sex intercourse is concerned, the oneness occurs metaphorically as love of another. The actual aloneness at the physical level is less than the oneness of masturbation. Women having sex together achieve orgasm and fluids may be exchanged

but to what purpose other than to be combined with sweat and washed away?

Men having sexual relations are even more foreign to nature as fluids combine in the anus or oral cavity for the end result of ejection.

Male and female coupling can have as a natural result, the birth of a child. The only birth that same-sex-coupling yields is death. As the metaphor of God, love and unity is expressed in the natural purpose of sex between man and woman as a union with the truth, the Father of Truth so also does the coupling of man on man unnaturally express an untruth, a union with the Father of Lies, the evil one, the Devil. To emphasize the truthfulness of this reflection, think about the common homosexual foreplay as prelude to anal intercourse and consider how repulsive and unnatural is the "rimming" of placing a man's tongue into the anal orifice of another man with the possibility of the tongue and mouth touching and ingesting the other man's fecal matter.

At root, sexuality pervades all aspects of existence. The interpretation of the meaning of such a pervasive phenomenon has to be a true interpretation. This interpretation must be passed on to our children in a convincing manner for only then will the truth set us free.

JOANNA
Thank you **CHRIS**, that was very enlightening. But now, let's get back to your marriage. Did you meet your future wife in DC?

JOHN
I met my future spouse shortly after coming to DC. The Pentagon had a picnic and I didn't have a date. I stood outside church before the 9:00 Mass and was hoping to meet someone I could invite

to the picnic. A little lady, cute and prim, appeared; I introduced myself and offered an invitation. She accepted and off we went.

At the picnic there was a vivacious gal opening beers (with a church key). I planted my date at poolside and visited with the church-key hostess. I was able to get a phone number. Later that day, I tried to seduce my date and failed. The next day, I called my future spouse, Nan, for a date and she said OK.

It was a rather strange date, because Nan had tried to find out who the new LTJG was at the Pentagon and wanted to beg off. Her Captain knew of me, but said "You made a date with a fellow-officer, you keep it." We packed off in my 1960 VW convertible and went to the Carton Baron concert on the Potomac. I spared no expenses and brought two six-packs of "Brown Derby" beer (.99 each) and rented a canoe.

Our relationship developed nicely as Nan was a lot of fun to be with and we had a lot of snickers. One night, I got laid. Pretty nice, as she was almost as virginal as I. I just remembered, it smelled great. I sniffed my finger all the way home. True love.

Well, she couldn't be hotter, just loved to fuck. One night, she wondered what my intentions were, and said,"Are we going to get married or what?" I said it might be fun and a good idea. I proposed shortly thereafter.

It's funny, the engagement period was rather pure and austere regarding sex- there wasn't much of it. We had a terrific wedding with a cast of thousands, champagne fountain, and great Pennsylvania honeymoon- alas, pretty stingy on the sex part. Funny how I never slept alone until I was married.

Life was a blast in DC. I met my spouse, who acquired the name of "plaintive" and is now Ex-spouse after close to 20 years of marriage. Before all that, she was just great and she was hot. Well, until we got married and then I had a hard time just getting any on my wedding night. We had brief rounds of sexual delight when it came time to produce offspring; she wanted to do it everyday. I was a major supplier of sperm.

We left DC and went west to find fame and fortune. I lucked into a swell sales job and still maintained my Navy Reserve status. It was at a Reserve meeting that I first saw hard core pornography.

The first really XXX movie I saw was in black and white, and the guy wore black socks. It was shown on an old Bell & Howell movie projector, using16mm film and I viewed it at a Naval Reserve meeting, would you believe it? I could not believe it when the screen projected a cunt filled in with a pumping engorged prick, sliding back and forth amid bouncing balls, and not the kind you follow when doing a sing-a-long. The panting in the audience was only surpassed by the moans on the screen.

We had our first child in California, a baby boy. The spouse immediately closed her legs and cunt for further activity from my pecker. At this time *Playboy* was not too risqué, but this centerfold with a Japanese cunt flourishing gigantic teats and a brief glimpse of shadowy cunt hairs, drove me to the bathroom to jack off. Wouldn't you know it, the spouse almost catches me with my pants at half-mast. I was embarrassed.

I really think that was one of the major problems with our marriage: lack of sex. Nan just wasn't interested. I also think that later on, drinking, job problems accelerated the process of "irreconcilable

194

differences". I think drinking started to influence my life, both my married life, limited sex life and business world when I turned 40. My evenings were mostly spent in the library, a room I finished off into a secluded den just off the family room, reading, listening to the stereo and sipping fine beverages from my "field bar." This was a wooden piece of furniture that supported a decanter, crystal glasses to match and had wooden sides cut out to hold one's favorite booze. In my case, it was George Dickel bourbon, Dewars scotch, and some brandy. These I sipped as my family sat in the next room watching TV. I would retire and find my spouse asleep. I would nudge her looking for some sex and get a "don't bother me" kind of response. I a semi-coma I would start to masturbate, trying not to let the gentle motion wake her, I'd be embarrassed. I think she knew what I was doing though, as occasionally she would grab my hand, not my dick, to stop the process. Just lovely.

I found that I was getting more and more morose, and communication was at a virtual standstill. Oh, I was cheery and bouncy in the morning, getting coffee for the wife, delivering it with a freshly picked gardenia from our yard. She would light a cigarette and continue primping; I might get a semi-smile. Upon our mutual departing for work I might be offered a cheek to peck. Big fucking hairy deal!

Problems with work developed. I obtained a rather big-deal position and wasn't able to hack it. I was demoted back to sales and I think it made a big difference in our relationship- from manager to sales, I was a loser. Nan was also experiencing difficulties. Earlier, she asked if we should have more children or should she go to work. The idea was to get a little piddly job, maybe with a company car, and get out of the house a few hours a day. Nothing that would interfere with domestic responsibilities etc. Well, she got a full

time job, became a sales manager and experienced the sexual discrimination prevalent big time in the 80's. She moped, I moped, didn't talk much except to whine and complain.

Things deteriorated. The kids, now in their teens, were little juvenile delinquents because they could get away with it. Nan and I were smokin' and drinkin' up big time, with rambling conversations, mostly about Nan's fantasies and discontent. She became excessively materialistic and stopped going to church altogether. She encouraged the children to pass on church attendance. I guess what did it, was one night over a rather sensuous meal at a fine Atlanta restaurant, I said to her: "You are a armor plated, ball-cutting machine." That was it.

We separated after almost 20 years of marriage, most of those as brother and sister who didn't get along too well. I was so horny I could shit. In two months I dated 25 girls and couldn't get to first base. I had a hard-on especially for a twenty-something who was an artist and smoked pot. I could have died to get her in bed, but she said she didn't have that special click for me. Back to *Hustler* and the hand jobs. I didn't really have any inclination to homosexual fantasies at this time, I was strictly heterosexual, or trying to be, about the only sex I was experiencing was with Merry Hand.

It's a funny thing about masturbation, the urge seems to come on strong when:

- I'm bored.
- I've had a hard day, stressed out, and want a drink, smoke and relax.

196

- I'm alone, and have to do something mental that I don't want to do, like required reading for work or school, juggling a schedule to accommodate interests in which I have none.
- Biologically, the day before my herpes acts up, or some other not understood cause.

I just have an urge to buy porno.

Bored and alone. If I'm with people and doing something interesting, yanking out my dick and jacking off would be an inconvenience. But if I'm bored, *isolated,* alone and have some porn, I get hot, stroke it and enjoy a great release. But do I really *feel* good about it afterward?

Woody Allen, a great satirist and actor, once said "the difference between dying alone and having sex alone is that people don't laugh at the former."

CHRIS

Perhaps self-love is OK, if it allows a diffusion of love to and for another person, and not a thing. Love of things still puts us squarely into ourselves and self-gratification. Selfishness seems a bit lifeless, useless, stale and tomorrow-less

What is the difference between LOVE and LUST?

LOVE is patient. *LUST* wants it now, like in Redneck foreplay: "On your back, bitch."

LOVE seeks others, shares, and wants the best for another. *LUST* doesn't give a shit.

LOVE gives life, perhaps new life, a baby. *LUST* might have a "love baby" (what a misnomer) that is a problem. "Wham, bam, thank you mam, have an abortion."

LOVE is something of value. LUST is fleeting as Shakespeare has said: "Tyrannical lust, unreasoned hunted, no sooner had than unreasoned hated."

JOHN
Yeah, right buddyroll. You try celibacy while married: it suxs.

The Farmer's Daughter was a triple X movie I watched back in the 70's at the Buckhead Art Theater in Atlanta. I had a secret desire to go downtown and watch a flick at the Blue Boy, which featured gay movies, but I was too embarrassed. This was one of the last full-length porno movies I watched and it was a humdinger. It started out with the farm boy lying on a bed eating a young girl's pussy, as she straddled over his face. At the same time, another girl was sucking off his beautifully shaped dick. This may have been the first time I really enjoyed looking at a young, full fleshed, engorged penis. The movie turned nasty as violence entered into it. Three hoodlums, one black, two whites, invaded the farmhouse at gunpoint and forced the farmer's daughters to take it up the ass. Much moaning and groaning as they were sodomized. The scene ended with the farmer getting forcibly blown by his daughter and his wife getting screwed by their son. You can see why this left me somewhat shaken. Oh yes, there were a couple of murders during this mayhem. This, I think was the beginning of the era of sex and violence in movies.

Even less satisfying, is the experience of the then quarter peek shows. A person would select what every kinky fancy turned him

on and sit in a closed booth, popping quarters into a box that activated a small screen for a few moments with XXX movies. The booth had a lot of cum shots on the wall, etc. Some of the booths provided paper towels, most didn't. I'd watch with a boner in my pants and finally jack myself off in my pants, hoping I wouldn't leave a big cum spot, wet, sticky and visible to all on my way out.

I didn't do this much, it felt too unclean. These places smelled bad. This was before the AIDS scare. All of these places disappeared around Atlanta before the 80's.

I did try a gay movie when I was in St. Paul, MN. It was okay, though I felt a little strange when I went into the men's room to take a leak. There was this guy sitting on a couch, also some guys hanging around the stalls, all of them looked pretty gruesome, and this was before the AIDS epidemic. I just couldn't imagine asking someone to suck me off in the toilet, or for that matter, sucking some else off sitting on the crapper. Actually, I sort of can imagine it and it makes my dick grow hard.

Hoping I wasn't gay, I sneaked into the next room where a regular heterosexual fuck scene was taking place, and found my attention was easily had. I didn't jack off in my pants though, but did enjoy a throbbing hard-on.

Today's movies of soft porn are really boring. Just a lot of faces huffing and puffing with an occasion glimpse of a bun or tit. Seldom see male genitalia or a twat. Just a lot of moans. I don't bother, and rather wish for the good old days at the Buckhead Art. They may be making a return, I noticed a sexual goods store opening on Peachtree St. just last month. The girlie show places have proliferated, so I expect the ethic patrol or vice squad may

no longer be on the hunt, hence the proliferation of cunt. At one time, it was just like Broadway, with XXX movies and sex stores back to back. Oddly enough, some of these establishments were located next to Sacred Heart Cathedral on old Ivy St. I use to go to confession at noon at Sacred Heart, and try to be chaste for a while.

I visited a new XXX store the other day. They've been outlawed here for over ten years and I guess some entrepreneurs are going to give it another go, especially since the nude dancer establishments have proliferated without much hassle. What caught my eye upon entering was a display of anal expanders. It is a device shaped like a butt plug, only made of rubber and expandable by squeezing air from a connected tube. It looked like it might be titillating, shoving that plug up my anus and pumping it up. I bet the sensation is neat, and could be all the more fun if some young guy was doing the pumping as a prelude to lubing up my asshole for receiving his young cock.

I sauntered by the XXX Gay mags, and reminisced how I use to ogle them in the past, with there slick covers displaying guys sucking each other off, cum splashed on their young faces. Since all the mags were sealed with plastic bags, I could just imagine the inside pages showing graphic rimming and sodomizing, my dick was getting hard. The high price, ranging from about $13 to $40 began to soften my dick. I looked at the for rent in private viewing room videos and wish I had the time and the courage to rent, sit and enjoy.

I rented a gay flick in Florida once, gosh it was lengthy. This guy comes over to another guy's pad and gets right down to eating his asshole out; I mean big time munching. I wish I could lick my

supper plate as clean as he licks this guys butt hole. After that he starts a slow languorous fuck. It goes on interminably, with the guy being fucked having his legs over this other guy's shoulders. The screen fills with a hot pole being shoved up and asshole, right to matching balls. My dick really got hard, and I wanted to join the countless thousands who shot their wads all over the booth I was sitting in and availed themselves of the paper towel roll. I resisted, though, didn't want to commit a mortal sin, I was just curious, that's all. I left the place a little sheepishly and rather exhausted, the music alone on these videos really wears you out.

I returned to my motel, dropped trousers and whacked off, couldn't help it, the images were just too strong. Thumpa, thumpa, thumpa.... whoosh.

My tastes have changed. Right now I'm looking at a porno mag called *Cock Wild*. There's this picture of a young good looking guy sucking the cock of a young kid while another dude has his dick about 1/2 way up his anus. The next picture is a close up and his dick is all the way up the young kid's ass, while the cocksucker is working the tip. I'd like to grab my own dick and flag it, but my conscience won't let me. I've a cucumber in the fridge, and would like to carve it into a humongous penis and suck it while I look at this picture, but my conscience won't let me. After simulating fellatio, I'd like to take the nicely carved cucumber and slowly, gently imagine that my asshole is the same as the kid in the picture, and let this young stud fuck me. My conscience won't let me. But who knows, maybe I'll do it anyway.

Boy, I like dirty movies. I would really like to have a collection at home on my VCR, but I'm too chicken. What if I should die and my kids find XXX gay movies on my shelf? It would be awful.

Also, I still have scruples about masturbating with pornography and don't consider it entirely guilt free, which is the next topic of our conversation.

There it lies, full of cum, nowhere to go. I look in the mirror at my limp dick and reflect on the pleasure I had of jacking off using a rubber.

Damn! It felt good, but why do I feel guilty. Isn't my dick just a joystick to give me release and pleasure?

What is there about talking dirty, watching sexy movies, fantasizing that is so damn yummmy, yet guilt ridden? Is it just that I'm a Roman Catholic and scrupulous, or do other non-Catholics feel the same way? I bet they do, but won't admit it.

CHRIS

Your remember from you seminary days the course you had in Christian Ethics. Thomas Aquinas argued from the natural law that the primary end of sexual union was procreation. The Church later added the procreation and education of children. If sexual activity did not accomplish this end it was wrong. It was unnatural. It was a sin. On this basis a whole moral theology developed that placed great emphasis on the act itself.

Charles E. Curran's book, <u>Faithful Dissent</u>, was foundational in understanding the problem of methodology used in noninfallible hierarchical teachings on sexual morality. In his book, <u>Tensions in Moral Theology</u>, he clearly explores the problem of biologism in the method of natural law interpretation of certain behavior in contrast to the legal or law model employed in social contexts. An

example of the latter would be in the morality of killing. "Thou shalt not kill" is interpreted that putting an armed aggressor to death such as in the case of war, or in the case of justifiable self-defense as not applicable. Circumstances and intent are taken into consideration in the law model of methodology, whereas in the former example of judging sexual morality, the law model is overridden by deontological absolute determinants of the natural law that some actions are intrinsically evil.

> "There can be no doubt that there are three important methodological differences between hierarchical Roman Catholic teaching on social morality and the official hierarchical teaching on sexual morality. Whereas the official social teaching has evolved so that it now employs historical consciousness, personalism, and a relationally-responsibility ethical model, the sexual teaching still emphasizes classicism, human nature and faculties, and a law model of ethics" (Curran: Tensions in Moral Theology.107).

The Pope's encyclical Veritatis Splendor, uses the deontological viewpoint of natural law to support various moral conclusions regarding human behavior. This is a fundamental premise supported by the magisterium (teaching office of the Roman Catholic Church) since the days of St. Thomas who placed reason under the order of nature:

> "Since the order of nature comes directly from God as its author, it assumes a priority and superiority over the order of reason which comes more immediately from the human person. St. Thomas maintains his position in the *Summa* when dealing with the morality of sexual matters.
>
> 'Reason presupposes things as determined by nature... so in matters of action it is most grave and shameful

to act against things as determined by nature'" (TT. II-II, q. 154. a. 12). (Gula, Richard M. SS, <u>What Are They Saying About Moral Norms</u>? New Jersey: Paulist Press,1982. 36).

"Following St. Thomas' principle that the most serious actions are those which go against nature, would have to conclude that masturbation is a more serious violation of chastity than incest, adultery, rape, or fornication ST. II-II, q. 154, as. 11, 12) Contemporary moralists do not understand nature as prescribing God's moral will. Nature provides the material with which we have to deal in a human way to promote the well being of human life. We discover what natural law requires by reason's reflection on what is given in human experience"(37 Gula) .

St. Thomas thought biologically that the sperm contained all the components of generativity and that the female egg was a passive component to nurture the male creative process. He even referred to sperm as a *homunculus* literally a "little man". Therefore, the "spilling of seed", masturbation was a grave evil because little men, potential newborns, were wasted.

"Sexual activities excluding procreation (Thomas classifies them in an order of ascending gravity: masturbation, marital contraceptive intercourse, homosexuality, bestiality) are sins against biological nature (*contra naturam omnis animalis* against the nature of animals). They are graver than the sins which do not exclude procreation (in ascendant degree of gravity: fornication, adultery, incest), because they go directly against God, the Creator who expresses his will in the biological nature. Therefore, in a certain sense they are even graver than sacrilege. (37 Gula)

Because incest would be open to procreation, it is considered less an evil than masturbation which is not open to procreation. This thinking shows how fallacious it is to judge the morality of an action strictly on the basis of its *perceived* conformance to biological law. Certainly the law of love and also of reason (common sense) are more severely disregarded by procreating a baby with your mother or sister than by violation of genital sexual activity's supposed preordained end of procreation. The nub of the whole argument is that there is a comfort zone in universal, immutable dictates that can serve as norms from which to reason conduct. It puts the legislature in control and confers power of interpretation and binding. Religion, *religare*, Latin for binding back, sometimes confers power through moralizing: "Do this, avoid this! This is sin, this is virtue!" because it complies with norms. The norms of morality are intrinsically, immutably set by God in the form of natural law, which is the eternal law made know to us by.....? Some say reason, and this would make it a circular argument. Some say by revelation interpreted by the *Magisterium* (teaching authority of the Roman Catholic Church) without error. Some say nature helps us understand God's purpose, but it is nature as reflected upon and reasoned by the human being that is the apex of nature. *God's glory is shown by man fully alive (St. Irenaeus d. 200AD circa).*

> To conclude, Jesus is the norm of morality and he gave us *his* law of love:

> "Love the Lord your God with your whole heart, soul and mind and love your neighbor as yourself" (Matt 22:37).

> This was first enunciated in Deuteronomy 6:4: "Hear, O Israel: The Lord is our God, the Lord alone. You shall love the Lord your God with all your heart, and with all your soul, and with all your might."

Jesus teaches the law of love by showing that one's love of God is irectly reflected in one's love of neighbor.

At heart, it is the Pope citing Scripture: "He who hears you, hears me" (Lk 10:16). It is the Pope, hungry for power and control, who states that he is infallible in his discernment of good and bad behavior because the Holy Spirit directs him. Even so, he bolsters his views by his interpretation of natural law by his reason supposedly enlightened by the Holy Spirit.

> "The reasonableness of the alternative positions becomes the theological source of new knowledge for the formulation of conscience. This is right in line with the natural law tradition, which has maintained that a moral conclusion is based on the reasons that support it, and not on the office of those who propose it. (Gula 101)

In writing to the bone, it's truly a both/and rationalization. The eternal law is expressed deep within the human person as the natural law, written in his/her heart which truly shows purpose and end which is in conformity to the will of God and hence, good.

It is a fundamental option of the reasoning person in the formation of his/her conscience to freely embrace God as the way, truth and life and with this horizon of faith, so shape his/her worldview and behavior. Pursuing this horizon leads to acts of behavior, which are loving, kind, just and truly good. Embracing the reverse, a denial and rejection of God as way, truth and life and directing one's horizon to oneself or other created thing is the fundamental option of idolatry and the actions and behavior issuing from this option are hard pressed not to be evil. "By their fruits you will know them" (Matt 12:33).

John Paul II in <u>Veritatis Splendor,</u> reaffirms the traditional concept of mortal and venial sins, and discerns that the Trentian doctrine of definition:

(1) grave matter.

(2) Full consent.

(3) Full knowledge can and does constitute mortal sin and a rejection of sanctifying grace with the rejection of eternal life.

This is still imagining grace to be "stuff" and "sin" to be a mark on the soul and harkens back to the times of Trent. A mortal sin, committed with the fundamental option of idolatry, and repeatedly committed can lead to this fundamental option and a deadening of conscience. Mortal and venial sin are not things and numbers to be taken to the confessional like dirty laundry and thus cleansed and removed. The actions are bad, the sins grave, but who is not guilty of sin? We listen to Jesus and by the grace of God, his free gift, we turn once again to our fundamental option and repent, ask and receive forgiveness. . It's not so much the act as it is the attitude. The "acts" (sins) we'll always have with us, it's how we respond to God's mercy and our determination to respond to his grace that really matters.

JOANNA

That kind of analysis is beyond my depth, but I do see that a guilty conscience can come from truly believing that masturbation with homoerotic pornography is sinful. But is this action a fundamental turning away from your belief in God? Are your rejecting him and worshiping your penis as a god? Or are you just obsessed, bored and mixed up over a sexually dissatisfying marriage and have developed a neurosis. Please continue on with your thoughts.

JOHN

Finally Ginger entered. Or rather I entered Ginger, a lovely blond who hadn't had a date for over a year. She was down on men, but for some reason, took to me and wanted to be fucked really bad. I think it was the ride on my motorcycle, the attention I paid to her and the gently squeezes on her thigh as we motored the North Georgia mountains. She literally, took me to bed, sucked me and pounced her red hot cunt on my really eager cock. She screamed, "**JOHN**, I'm coming all over you!" And she did...wow. It was the first time I had a women since I was married. I was one of those faithful dudes. If that cunt I was married to did this even once, things might have been different. She was just a man emasculating, armored plate, frozen cunt that had her own agenda and it didn't include *moi*.

Ginger helped me gain some self-esteem. I felt like a man once again, and a man who was attractive and wanted. She suggested a weekend at a motel and I jumped at the idea. We had a lovely pastel room with adjacent hot tub jacuzzi. What a beautiful woman, lying there with the prettiest, softest cunt, I just wanted to touch it. It was tucked in between gorgeous buns, we fuck and fucked. Alas, we both realized fucking was our only bond and our relationship dimmed.

Shortly after that I met several gals and was unsuccessful at getting laid. One in particular was eighteen and after 3 Manhattans I thought I could score. She went home. I met another girl, probably about 30's and somewhat attractive, she went home with me the first night. She kept saying, higher, higher etc. she loved to fuck. Once again, that was it, just a good lay and some companionship.

JOANNA

So you were getting laid and enjoying female companionship. Did homosexual thoughts and masturbation tend to go away?

JOHN

Because of the lack of any love involved in this sexual activity, the concentration on my dick still led to homosexual fantasies.

Some time ago, I stopped by Joe Bikinis shop on Piedmont. It's not there anymore, but it use to supply the snap off bikinis for the nude dancers, both for the girls and boys. Just before they closed, I was digging through a "sale" box of goodies and came up with a male stripper bikini, a thong with a pouch in brilliant hues of chartreuse, pink and green. I asked Matt, the young clerk, if this was me, he agreed it was. I also found a gay man's bathing suit in hot orange with a little yellow tag on the rear which read "Pan Dulce", which I think is French for "All Sweet". Matt thought this was me also. The list price for these treasures came to about $50. They were on sale for five dollars each, I bought both fantasies.

The bathing suit reminded me of a visit I paid to a gay apartment complex located in Ansley. It was about noon, and I was traveling by the pool on my way to the rental office. I was working for a sign company at the time, and I was going to call on the Office Manager and inquire if they might need our services. As I drove by the pool, I notice about a dozen young men lounging about, working on their tans and erections. One in particular caught my eye. He was lean and blond, probably late teens or early twenties. He had on a swim suit similar in design and cut to the one I purchased at Joe's. He was chatting with a dude, combing his long blond hair in a sort of feline way, and thrusting his hips out, which outline his long tool lovingly displayed in tight spandex. My dick started to grow hard.

I parked, and moved to a picnic table with some paperwork and occupied myself with writing, all the while studying the gay pool manscape. There were a lovely assortment of buns. Blond boy was gesturing to his nipples and cock to his attentive pool pal. Another Adonis had stepped out of the pool and was drying off. I'd like to suck him off, if he asked me. He put on a pair of shorts, much like a girl does when she leaves the pool and doesn't want to display her lovely buns and snatch barley covered by a spandex thong. In the process, his penis bobs up and down before disappearing behind the zipper of his shorts. These thoughts are making my cock grow hard as I continue in my boredom, in front of the mirror after my shower.

Nothing to do, really and no place to go exactly. Standing in front of the mirror and looking at myself, what a lovely cock! Think I'll touch it, hmmm. I've a long, thin brown shoelace, think I'll tie under my balls and around the shaft of my lovely penis. Hmmmmm, that feels good. I'm getting a little turgid, I like it.

Think I'll put on both the thong, and the "Pan Dulce", hmmmm looks great. My swollen, tied up cock bulges even better that the young poolside studs. I sit on my bed and carefully pull on a pair of black pantyhose, which I acquired one Halloween for a costume. I went as a cheerleader, and enjoyed the sensation of dressing as a girl; I do have attractive, hairless long legs. I have to be careful in putting on the pantyhose, for they tear easily. Boy, would I like to tear into some young boy-ass. I'm getting hot and want to fuck a male asshole. My cock is throbbing and I begin to undress in front of the mirror. First the black pantyhose, is your cock or clit aroused? I peel off the layers of spandex and untie the shoelace around my long, beautiful penis and cup my balls gently. Ever try fucking yourself? It's not as hard as trying to suck yourself off, but

just as impossible for the average 6 to 8 inch cock. In order to suck yourself, or jam your tool up your own ass, I would think you need about 10 inches of prod. Anyway, I take my penis, which has lessen somewhat in erection and rub it between my legs, between my right thigh, and testicle, gently slipping it toward the rear. With a little effort I can almost put the head of my dick in my ass. It's close, I can feel it touch and almost insert. I'm getting really hot now, I turn around and look in the mirror, I see my balls, my hand thrusting my dick very close to the orifice of my anus. Darn, wish I had a couple of more inches, I'd be home, baby. Right up my ass! I settle for a gentle masturbation just between by balls and asshole. It's a tender spot and both my dickhead and the spot enjoy the steamy sensation. Pow, a juicy blop of jizz spurts out on the spot and feels warm and sticky. Guess I'll have to take another shower, if I'm not too weak.

Whew, after all this I think I'll have a glass of Burbon on the rocks. You know the two seem to go together, fucking and drinking. Previously, when I smoked, the three went together: buy a pack of butts, a glass of Bourbon and some porn- strip down, grab your cock and lets go.

JOANNA
You mentioned drinking several times. Do you think you might have another compulsion?

JOHN
Maybe so. I had cut down considerably. My roomy who I was sharing an apartment with, did a good job on the vodka. I thought *he* was drinking too much. His health, job and finances all went into the shiter. Not a happy life. He died.

I didn't notice my drinking becoming a steady item until it reached a pretty consistent six to eight drinks a day. This is also when I noticed a desire of homosexual pornography and masturbation in preference to normal heterosexual sex and female porno. The effect of alcohol tends to isolate me, make me think of my dick and throw me into intemperate desire of sensual pleasures, avoiding work or any kind of mental activity other than leafing through porn books. I loss a lot of time and energy. I whack off so much that I'm exhausted and don't feel good. Everything is a bother and effort. People irritate me. I have little interest in anything, I'm bored, really bored. I have just enough energy to get to the pity pot.

JOANNA

Let me share with you a review I read on a book entitled: *Moderate Drinking* by Audrey Kishline.

> "The Big 6/8, six the easy way, 8 the hard way! A common call heard at he craps tables in Vegas. For me it was the number of drinks I was daily consuming. Not just carefully poured out shot glass drinks, but robust poured from the 1.75 plastic liter of $9.88 Vodka until about and add a dash of Cranberry Juice Cocktail for color and flavor.
>
> I'd have about two or three of these manly Cape-Codders when getting home from work. I'd change into tennis togs and meet the guys for a set of doubles. Larry brought the beer, so we'd have a few during and after the match. Dinner would follow preceded by a Gimlet or two, and them either beer or wine with dinner. A little relaxation after dinner, a scotch while reading my book. Gosh, I must have passed out in my chair, it's 2:30 am.
>
> The Big 6/8 was starting to increase to more like 10 or 12 drinks a day, which seemed to be becoming

shorter. My energy level and consciousness departed with my last toddy for the body around 8:30 p.m..

Any book I read about discerning if I'm an alcoholic I read with a bias? Not me! I don't want to go to AA, I can handle it, I seldom have a hangover, I'm not late for work, it's just that I don't seem to have the energy I once had, and I have very little patience. I'm angry a lot and my personality seems to be changing. Also my eyes are seldom clear, bright and shiny, the whites are always red-veined and the rest of the eye has a rather glazed, dull look. My problem solving abilities and memory seem to be less than what they once were.

Well after reading this fine little book of 166 pages, I took the first step and admitted I had a bad habit and hoped it was not too late to do something about it on my own.

JOHN
Pretty good advice. I think giving up the booze is a lot harder than giving up smoking. I humbly admit I use to smoke like a furnace, anything that burned found its way into my mouth. But you know, words are powerful. One day a friend of mine asked me if I inhaled my cigars. I gave the usual response: "Oh, sometimes." He replies: "Your lungs must look like cork." I quit shortly thereafter, and found that there is life after giving up smoking.

I try to drink moderately now, but if I'm not careful, I'll drink six or eight drinks. Drinking may have to go the way of smoking unless I can control it better.

CHRIS
You mentioned guilt feelings?

JOHN

I'm Roman Catholic, and still have qualms about masturbation. Oh, I've read varying opinions trying to justify occasional whacking off, but when I reach a point where I did last night, I have to throw my crutches out, go to confession, and try, try again to adopt a more disciplined life style. It's just the way I am, and it is a burden.

Last night, I opted for masturbation in preference for live sex with my girl friend. Oh yes, I've been divorced for many years and that's why I have complete liberty, or shall we say, license, to drop my trousers and pull my pud anytime I please. Even when I do have sex with her, we do it doggie style, fantasizing that I'm screwing her in the ass. She seems to enjoy it though, and I truly love her and am sorry I have to use this deception in order to get a hard-on.

It all comes down to my sexuality and preference of using objects as a means of orgasm. Even my cutting out dicks, assholes etc. and masturbate on them indicates that I don't want sex with a person, I'd rather isolate the activity and use masturbation solely for my pleasure and release.

Well, after she went home, and I had a considerable quantity of alcohol, I dug up my recently thrown away Gatorade bottle, a hot dog which I warmed in the microwave and stripped to my nice black bikini cut briefs. I started reading porn stories, accompanied by pictures from *Rump*. I put the hot dog in some Vaseline slowly threaded up my ass while looking at a picture of a young boy getting dildoed. The hot dog felt good, but wasn't stiff enough to really do the job. I left in partially inserted while I put the Gatorade bottle over my somewhat erect stick. I squeezed the bottle, pretending the vacuum sucking effect was some Adonis sucking me off. I had too much to drink and had difficulty in coming, but eventually

I came. I looked at the small amount of cum on my hand and thought about licking a little of it to see what it tasted like. I always think about doing this before I come, but never do it afterward, except once. It tasted a little like chalk.

I passed out, and awoke a bit later only to be obsessed again with my porn and pud. What a site, trying to whack off a limp, used up prick, but the heat in my loins, urges me on...whack-a-whack-a-whack. Cum and go. Go back to sleep.

CHRIS
We talked a little bit about what constitutes morality for sexual actions. If the action is open to procreation, from a natural law view, the action is appropriate and good.

But is there all there is to sex? Biological ends? I think not. I suggest that a sexual act has moral good if it expresses integration of human relationships such as: other-enriching, honest and faithful, life-serving, joyful, socially responsible and self-liberating.

Your actions don't seem to measure up. Your masturbation is actually hedonistic, self-seeking pleasure. Your homosexual tendencies come from boredom with heterosexual sex. You are concentrating solely on what give you a rush. I would venture to say, your next step might be child pornography, perhaps even sadism and bestiality. Anything at all to satiate your libido and lust.

JOHN
Yikes! You may be right. What am I to do?

JOANNA
Well obviously you plan of confession and trying again, haven't had long term good results. Maybe you ought to forego the guilt aspect

and develop a different perspective of love, forgiveness, tolerance and try to come to a mature sexual response to your drives.

JOHN

Yeah buddy. I can't let it go. In some pornographic literature, men seem to like anal penetration. It's like they are an insatiable woman, able to receive dick after dick and yet remain ready for more. They think that getting penetrated is really super satisfying. One porno vignette I read describes the guy's lover putting an electric dildo up his ass while blowing him. He turns on the dildo and creates all kinds of jumpy, exquisite sensations from asshole to prostrate to balls and cock, which is being suck with great vigor. The suckee cums with load after load of man cream and then spreads them for his sucker to insert his prod.

Other porn describes "Shemales" those people who look and act like a woman, but when they get to the crotch, there's a penis and balls. So, is there some kind of hang up here? Has blatant forms of feminism distorted male sexuality to the point of some thinking they are both male and female, or others thinking they are trans-sexual? Or has the relentless search for amusement in masturbation led to fantasies that include any hole, male, female, dog or cat, chained or unchained.

Identity, right now I identify myself with my dick. As I'm typing this I am looking at a little picture I've framed in a small 2"x3" frame of a guy's asshole. He's spreading his cheeks and displaying a young, succulent, anus slightly ringed with hair. His balls and cock are dangling down between his legs and my cock grows hard. I'd like to whip out my dick and start beating it, imaging alternately that I'm sucking him off from below and sticking my cock up his young ass. But I'm liable to shoot cum all over my keyboard and

that would be a stick mess. Also, my girl friend is coming over and if I jack off, I won't be able to do much later on, and that would be unfair to her.

As I ponder the image and practice a modicum of self-control, I reflect that there is nothing remotely resembling love in regarding an object and "making love" to it. Jacking off and making love are not the same. Actually, using a woman as a hole is not making love either, it's jacking off using an object. You know, my 2"x3" frame is small and only shows the genitalia I'm interested in. It's an object. Could be a picture of a disassociated cunt or female asshole, although the balls and cock would be missing in most cases. I find I like boys privates as objects to girls' cunts and boobs. The male body is more erotic.

By this time you may think I'm a queer. I like to think of myself as confused, and not really knowing why. Maybe for sake of saving face, I could call myself a bi-sexual, although I've never had sex with another man.

CHRIS

Mother Theresa had an interesting message that she sent to Beijing on the occasion of the U.N. women's conference held there in 1995.

> "All God's gifts are good, but they are not the same. God created all people to love and be loved, but God also created man and woman to be different.
>
> A woman's love is one image of the love of God, and a man's love is another image of God's love. Woman and man complete each other, and together show forth God's love more fully than either can do alone. Woman and man complete each other, and together

show forth God's love more fully than either can do alone.

God told us, 'Love your neighbor as yourself.' So first I am to love myself rightly, and them to love my neighbor like that. But how can I love myself unless I accept myself as God has made me? People who deny the differences between men and women deny the truth of their own identities. They cannot love themselves, and they end up sowing division between people rather than loving them."

JOHN

Yeah buddy. As long as we're on the subject of deviation, what do you think about having sex with children? Pederasty, why does it sound so nasty? Because it is. By definitions pederasty means sexual love of boys, or more specifically, the sexual relations between a man and a boy. I'm not competent to explore pedophilia, the sexual desire in an adult for a child, as a matter of fact, I can hardly spell the word. However, I would like to explore the desire to masturbate over kiddy-porn, or erotic pictures of children.

A graphic, soft-porn version for example, would be Calvin Klein underwear ads. There's one in particular were a young girl is prone, with her CK jean skirt hiked up to reveal the white strip of panties covering her young twat. Geesssh, it's an instant hard-on.

For the masturbator, there is always the desire to get new and more erotic pictures to fire up the imagination and increase the ecstasy of whacking off. After a person tires of twats, maybe the fantasy of sucking dick and anal intercourse provides an interesting, more exciting alternative. But what about a small, not yet developed, little cock and balls. Wouldn't it be fun to play with them, cause the penis to erect, even though its immaturity would not permit

orgasm? And after exciting such innocence, why not image, leading the boy to touch myself, play with my enormous organ of pleasure, tell him that his will be like mine some day. Encourage him to suck me. Play with his small, little rear end; gently insert my finger, maybe even the end of my dick.

There is no length to which the lust inflamed imagination will go to in order to produce excitement in the groin. Bring on the boys!

JOANNA
Whew! Whoa boy, let's take a break, call in **CHRIS** and get it together. I believe when we first started this conversation you mentioned something about seeking the truth and having an agenda something beyond titillation and making some money form the sale of this thinly disguised porno.

JOHN
You're right, let's call in **CHRIS** and have a three-way dialogue on my obsession. You know it is disordered and if I keep on, I'm liable to eat, live and sleep sexual deviations.

CHRIS
Let's tell a little story to illustrate a very important point in trying to overcome masturbation that has gotten out of control.

There once was a gent who was going to Detroit. He packed a map in his briefcase, and when he arrived in Detroit, to his chagrin, he had packed a map of Chicago! No matter how *hard he tried*, he could not find the street he was looking for by using the map he packed. He then thought, I'll just have a positive attitude about this. So what if I can't find the street, I just do something else, go someplace else, what does it matter. I'll find the place next trip, etc. etc. As one can see without the right map, the actions of trying

219

harder and the mind-set of positive attitude are of little value and don't get the job done. He needs the right road map to arrive at where he wants to be.

JOHN

I can appreciate what you're saying by trying harder to overcome an obsession. For many years, the priest in the box (Roman Catholic confessional) would always admonish that to avoid the occasion of sin, I.e. porno and *try harder.* So I would dutifully throw out my porno, which I had already done before coming to confession, say my penance, and try harder with a fresh start to avoid playing with myself. This would work for typically 6 to 8 weeks, then compulsively I'd trot down to the Newsstand and pick up a cello bag of gay porno and whack off.

It wasn't always gay literature; this didn't start until my 40's. Before I always would beat off with girlie mags. Then I got interested in both. I couldn't decide whether I preferred boys or girls, or both. Now, it's pretty much guys that turns me on. Although I still enjoy looking at females, their bodies are certainly beautiful, but seldom do they make my dick grown hard.

I guess it's the transition from true love of another sexually, to just wanting the solitary splendor of pulling the pork that makes masturbation desirable. Sex objectified, isolated and enjoyed through the senses and imagination in a nice irresponsible, immature safe fashion seems available and fun, wacka-wacka-wacka (www).

Perhaps it's the same with overcoming hedonistic masturbation that can occur at any age, but seems to be particularly attractive as one approaches mid-life, you know, the Dirty Old Man syndrome. The harder I try, the more obsessed I become with beating off. I

can adopt a positive attitude about the thing, but I'm just kidding myself, because if I have that book of boy's butts stashed away in my closet, I'll be looking at it again with the usual results of www. What I really need is a different map, a different perspective on the act.

I've tried to desensitize myself by hanging a rather erotic picture of a lovely strawberry blonde bending over a Porsche with a wrench. She's wearing a tight, revealing jumper, cut just above her firm cheeks, showing just a hint of soft down. Her lovely hair is highlighted and she is wearing no hose and white spike heels. This use to make my dick grow hard, but after constant exposure, I grew use to it, and now I look at it admiringly and without a hard-on. I'm trying this with a small framed picture of a young lad spreading his cheeks, showing his sphincter and lightly downed balls and tip of his cock, as he bends over. Now this makes my dick grow hard writing about it, but in actual practice, I have this framed picture on my bathroom sink, and look at it when I'm there. I judiciously put it in the vanity under the sink when I'm not there, as quests may think it a bit weird. I find that as I grow accustom to this most erotic gay pose, I am beginning to be desensitized to it. I've thrown out my other porn, because I know as I flip rapidly through many color pictures of naked men, I'll want to fantasize and jack off.

CHRIS

Earlier I mentioned the concept to *grace*, God's help by way of his very life within us. This grace can help us develop a new horizon, or worldview that gives us a *both/and* perspective of harmony and balance in nature. To view sex as the lust of unrestrained passion is really immature and not an adult activity that allows us to think of others, love others, be a mature Christian adult. **Maturity is a process of thinking of something and someone besides self.**

When it comes to sin, I don't think it's so much the action itself, but the mind-set that prompts and commits to the action. For example, premeditated murder is a more grievous offense that a murder committed in the heat of passion. Still the action of murder is objectively wrong, a distortion so to speak, because you distorted another existence into non-existence, but the enormity of the sin is the subjective adherence to it, the commitment of self to the act, you really wanted to blow this person's brains out, thought about it, planned it and executed it without regard for anything else.

Masturbation is a habit, like any other habit. It's almost like smoking. Nicotine triggers a chemical function in the brain that says: "This feels good, let's do it again." Same with orgasms, or the anticipation of orgasms. Let's face it, we'll all have sexual desires until we are dead. True, some people are walking death, and probably haven't had a hard-on in years, but these souls are the exception. It's a lot more effective to handle sexuality, our needs and desires from a calm world view of maturity and the realization that trying harder to avoid jacking off only excites to obsession.

JOHN

Tell me about grace, how can it help me develop this mature worldview you are describing.

CHRIS

Let me just repeat my definition of grace: **Grace is the love of God being perfected in us. It is the power and wisdom that takes the reality of positive and negative entities and through a paradoxical process produces a *both/and* results in the actualization of good.**

The action of grace is expressed by the Prophet Ezekiel in the Old Testament:

> "I will sprinkle clean water upon you to cleanse you from all your impurities, and from all your idols I will cleanse you. I will give you a new heart and place a new spirit within you, taking from your bodies your stony hearts and giving you natural hearts." (Ezekiel 36:25-26).

What a wonderful book the Bible is when we are searching for the truth. Our bodies are our tents that carry us in our journey through life. When we masturbate using pornographic pictures (graven images, idols), we become one with the images through our imagination and commitment to lusting after a picture of an orifice into which we spill semen. As we look at the sticky webs of fluid between our fingers, on our stomach and legs, we feel relieved, but at the same time, guilty. We are abusing our tent and we know it. Spiritual thoughts are 10,000 miles away and we want to keep it that way, but deep down there's a nagging. As Francis Thompson in the *Hound of Heaven*, put it so compellingly:

> "With unhurried chase and unperturbed pace, deliberate speed, majestic instancy, they beat- and a Voice beat more instant than the Feet-'All things betray thee, who betrayest Me.'"

The love of God begins its invasion, not like an army but like a gently breath of air. The Holy Spirit, the love personified between Father and Son, floats like the feather in *Forrest Gump*, if we try to grab it, the feather moves away beyond reach. If we let it descend, it lands gently in our palm. The Spirit can be like a gentle zephyr or a mighty, raging wind. It can be a purifying cleansing stream, crystal clear, cool to the touch and gently washing our tents whiter

than snow. The breath and power of God ignites our soul, fires our intellect so that we can now see clearly. We thirst for this Spirit of true love. We allow her entrance. We come to know her better through reflection on her stories in the Bible, especially *The Book of Wisdom, Proverbs, Ecclesiates and the Psalms.*

JOHN

I can see where true love helps me correct my living a lie. I respect my tent, and the tent of others. I perceive that whacking off on a picture of a blown up twat, or a bent over rear are indeed very pleasurable and will probably remain so until my dick falls off, but realize its a lie and not in my best interests, or in the interests of my fellow pilgrims in this journey of life. Masturbation, cuts me off, isolates me, and makes my heart grow as hard as my dick.

This hard, throbbing dick is a tool for satisfying a loving cunt. Typically, we are married to the cunt, but the woman we are married to is not just a life support system for a cunt, and neither am I a life support system for a dick! There's more to life than jacking off.

CHRIS

The Spirit will calm you and help you to realize the truth, the truth of love. And then she will penetrate you like no man ever could and plant her seeds of wisdom that bear the fruit of patience, courage, kindness, love and joy. She brings with her, temperance, prudence, self-control and harmony. We have the courage to change.

JOHN

As long as we're talking about the Bible, I have a question. Do you think that Jesus masturbated? Was Mary, his mother, always a virgin? Did Joseph, her husband, have sexual relations with Mary?

Did Jesus have sex with Mary Magdalene? What does God think about sex? What part does sex play in God's plan and design of things? Is sex dirty? What about sexy thoughts, perversions, such as getting sucked off by a 6 year old girl? Or how about putting some Vaseline on a tender young boy's asshole and sticking your engorged dick fully into it? Are these products of a sick mind, or is your dick getting hard just thinking about it?

Yes, my dick is getting hard just thinking about it, but you know, there's more to life than smoking, drinking, lusting and orgasms. What? Life without these things? *Unthinkable*!

I suppose some are more inclined to sex and it's many dimensions than others. And, there are competing interests that occupy the mind and body. When one is entirely taken up with a project, an interest such as working on a car, restoring classic motorcycles, engrossed in a fascinating novel, thoughts of masturbation are nowhere in sight. It's only when one is finished being involved and is tired, or when one is thinking about a task that is a pain in the ass and he or she would rather stick hot needles in the eye than do this thing, that lustful ideas present themselves as alternatives. Perhaps even after stepping out of the shower and viewing oneself in the bathroom mirror does the idea enter the mind of playing with such a pretty dick, or massaging those gorgeous balls and pretending that some young Adonis is standing behind you, rubbing your cock, rubbing his cock up your crack, wanting to penetrate, to fill your crack with man cream. Is your cock getting stiff, mine is.

I wonder if Jesus, after a day with the crowd, stifling, pushing in on him like we see in middle east movies, the crowds of people shouting, pushing, density, hot sweating bodies, a sea of noise and need, I wonder if Jesus, when he reclined, had some refreshment,

maybe a cup of wine, I wonder if his hand involuntarily reached down and massaged his genitals?

Did Jesus catch the sight of Mary Magdalene bending over to lift or get something, and notice the curve of her hips, the smooth contour of her behind, and did he get an erection?

In the rock musical *Jesus Christt Superstar*, Mary Magdalene sings a song *I don't know how to love him*. Did she have desires for Jesus sexually? Did Jesus desire her?

CHRIS

Jesus was truly a man, and as a man he was sexual. We are told by Scripture that he was tempted in all things, but that he did not sin. And what is sin anyway. One interpretation is that sin is a condition of unbelief, of unfaith. Basically, a condition of idolatry where the creature, refuses to acknowledge God in his or her life, and prefers the created to the Creator. Sin is a distortion.

Much of your illustrations and rather frank talk about cocks, assholes, cum etc. is probably a distortion. I don't think that jacking off in the bathroom is bringing you closer to a relationship with Jesus Christ. By the same token, I don't think that Jesus used masturbation as a means of drawing closer to his Father. I'll bet that he had wet dreams as a boy and that like all kids probably masturbated without fully realizing how solitary sex is a distortion from sexuality that is life serving, other enhancing, holistic and a deep symbol of love and creativity. Once realizing the dimensions of his sexuality, its purpose in God's plan and realizing the distortion and perversion that can occur by following the suggestions of the Father of Lies, the old adversary, Satan, I don't think Jesus

followed the path we so often take in sensual gratification without responsibility or concern for purpose. It just doesn't seem right.

Regarding Mary, his mother and Joseph his earthly dad and guardian, I find nothing contradictory in thinking they had a great sex life and some additional children. On the contrary, celibacy and virginity are so unnatural, that I find these conditions to be as much of a distortion as frank perversity. I'm afraid I have little respect for vowed celibacy. It's about as natural as cutting off ones balls and becoming a eunuch. It's a distortion. However, if someone wants to voluntarily (not mandated) choose celibacy, perhaps this can be done without consummate narcissism and selfishness. I don't know?

JOHN
You know **CHRIS**, I talked to a sex therapist regarding masturbation and I referred to it as *self abuse*. He corrected me: "No, no, no, you've got it wrong! The term is 'self-love', not 'self-abuse'. Self-abuse is an old outdated term for masturbation used by some sort of fundamentalists or Catholics."

This sex therapist that I spoke with, may have a point. He thinks that masturbation is healthy and has no guilt association because it's merely fantasy. So, the question that is posed: is masturbation both good and bad, or is it either good or bad?

Fundamentalists, quoting the incident of Onan in the book of Genesis, chapter 38, where he "spills his seed on the ground" and Catholics referring to Thomas Aquinas who thought that the seed contained complete human beings and therefore very sacred, both think that masturbation is gravely evil.

My thinking is that masturbation is fun. But sometimes fun can be dangerous. A single act of jacking off, not as a habit, or as a function similar in value to taking a crap, can be integrated into a healthy perspective. But the danger lies in masturbation becoming habit knit. For example, take smoking. I'm just kidding myself if I buy a pack of cigarettes and say, I'll just smoke one. Or, just a couple a day. Phooey, I'm kidding myself. Nicotine says to my brain, "Yummmy good, do it again!" And I'm right back on it, smoking at least a pack a day and turning my lungs to cork. That's an addiction, and every little wisp of smoke does its woeful deed in the tender little cells of my breathing apparatus. It's just no good. Smoking is not a "both/and" kind of thing, it's <u>either</u> quit (no smokes at all) <u>or</u> eventually walk around with an oxygen tank pulled after you as you feebly walk with tubes up your nose. Not a lot of fun and definitely bad for your golf game.

So anyway, daily beating off can be compared to the nasty, harmful habit of smoking. Look at an ashtray full of butts and ashes, and look at the cum on your hand after jacking off. In both instances you want to clean up. If you don't buy into this kind of thinking, it's okay, it's pretty shallow anyway, and I'm no expert, just wanted to get you thinking. Hey, if you read this book and give up smoking you'll save the price of the book in a couple of days. Also you may have nicer later years still being able to breath without assistance.

Either/or thinking about masturbation can cause odd results. After nine years in the seminary avoiding deliberate masturbation, I found that I was jacking off in my sleep.

After 19 years of a frigid marriage, I found I was jacking off in my sleep, or when wifey was out, I might get off on a copy of *Cosmopolitan.* Now that I'm single for 11 years, but in a very

committed relationship with a lovely woman, yet living apart, I find that I no longer jack off in my sleep, but now and then, get some porn and play around with myself, sometimes preferring gay porno with self-stimulation to regular sex.

I read something recently that said homosexual orientation could be due partially to lack of spermatogenesis or lack of sperm production. Perhaps my vasectomy of 15 years ago has influenced sperm production, and has strengthened a proclivity towards homosexuality. Actually though, burying my face in another man's crotch wouldn't smell so good. I just like to fantasize with porno, the actual real activity would scare me, what would I say? "Gosh, that's a nice dick. May I suck it for you?" And the idea of actually sticking my tongue down his throat, or around and in his asshole, choke, makes me gag.

You know, cunnilingus, or licking the cunt, is pretty neat and tastes good too. It's very sweet, like honey. I never tasted another man's cum, but tried my own just out of curiosity. It was very bland and tastes a little like chalk.

CHRIS

No, I don't think a vasectomy would increase your homosexual desires. When it comes to gays, I believe there are some folks who are just naturally oriented to the same sex. If that's the case, it's natural for them, and if we follow Thomas Aquinas with his theorizing about the morality of actions are determined by achieving their natural end as reflected by reason on the Eternal Law...well, they are just doing what comes naturally. There are others, like you, who become gay, bisexual or transsexual through the desire for titillation. For the desire for perversion, unnatural sex etc, merely to heighten sexual pleasures without responsibility

other than having a "good time." This is acquired homoeroticism and could come from an evil bent of mind. Let's take a good, hard look at *evil*. Hard core, rotten evil. *SIN*, another name for evil. What is it? It is an attitude. "Man, that boy has an attitude!" Whoa, you say," I know what sin is, it's like murder and cheating, screwing someone else's wife, shit like that, y'know." These actions are the consequence of sin. Oh sure, they are bad actions, but they aren't the root of the matter. Sin is an attitude of UNFAITH. A person who does not believe in God. This person thinks that he made himself. If he isn't that ridiculous, he thinks that he just happened by chance, or something, and that he better make the best of getting all he can before he croaks. If somebody mentions "God" to him or her, (figure on the male pronoun being inclusive of female as well, I'll go ape shit doing him or her, s/he etc. fuck it) he'll say "Well, not too relevant, I mean, how can their be a God when I see all the shit that's going on. What kind of God permits deformed babies, disasters of nature, terrorist actions etc. I don't need a God like that." Or, this person may say "Sure, it's a nice idea, I need it for my kids and it's good for business. I like to be seen in church from time to time etc.

Faith, or belief in a Divine Creator who has a plan and whose love for us brought us into existence is the cornerstone of good actions. Belief helps us to align our priorities and actions with truth. The truth of our being, our purpose in life and where we are destined to go. Scripture tell us of a God who sent his son, Jesus Christ (Jesus in Hebrew means Yahweh saves, and Christ means the anointed, or chosen one) to save (make whole, heal) us. The bottom line and net, net of our existence is to believe what Christ has said, believe in the promises of God, and that he has the power to accomplish what he said he would do. It is this: Love

God with your whole heart and soul, your neighbor as yourself. We obey God's will because we accept belief in him. Jesus main message was to proclaim his Father's love for us and to lead us to the kingdom of God. The Kingdom is beginning right now, day by day, as we grow in grace and love for God and his creations, love for one another and ourselves.

How does masturbation fit into all this? It could stem from a state of unbelief and accompany many other evil activities caused by this state. The state of unbelief is a conscious effort and mind-set that excludes God or light. Darkness and evil are preferred. Lies and untruth seep in and exchange truth about God for a lie: they worship and serve what God has created instead of the Creator himself

> "Because they do this, God has given them over to shameful passions. Even the women pervert the natural use of their sex by unnatural acts. In the same way the men give up natural sexual relations with women and burn with passion for each other. Men do shameful things with each other, and as a result they bring upon themselves the punishment they deserve for their wrongdoing.
>
> Because those people refuse to keep in mind the true knowledge about God, he has given them over to corrupted minds, so that they do the things that they should not do. They are filled with all kinds of wickedness, evil greed, and vice: they are full of jealousy, murder, fighting, deceit, and malice. They gossip and speak evil of one another, they are hateful to God, insolent, proud, and boastful; they think of more ways to do evil; they disobey their parents; they have no conscience; they do not keep their promises, and they show no kindness or pity for others. They know that God's law says that people who live in this

way deserve death. Yet, not only do they continue to do these very things, but they even approve of others who do them" (Romans 1:26-32).

So, masturbation could just be symptomatic of much greater evil. Just don't shrug it off. Look beyond for other causes than just an occasional whack off to release tension or the give into lewd thoughts. If your beating off is an obsession, it may be part of a more harmful disposition to evil, or this very obsession, left unchecked may lead to greater unfaith and cause a deep isolation and commitment to unlove.

Before leaving topic of evil, a disease commonly associated with gay people is the AIDS virus.

Got Aids Yet? Not a very nice acronym, but like all acronyms, there's a ring of truth to it. The AIDS virus is carried in the blood and other fluids and in the male sperm. So, if another person ingests infected sperm, there you have it, AIDS transmission efficient and effective. Effective for what? Effective for death, dear heart.

Oh, there are a lot of non-gay AIDS victims, and these folks really got a bad rap. Some people consider AIDS as the avenging angel sent by God to get the gays. I don't think so. Some cheer it as a way to reduce the black population. I don't buy than one either. It's literally a damn fucking virus that I hope goes the way of polio and we get rid of the menace.

I would like to use a comparison, however, between the pathology of AIDS and the pathology of sin. Both are a disease of the body and the spirit. The above figure represents a wandering HIV+ cell in search of a victim white cell. Having found the victim, the HIV+ locks on, penetrates and injects the virus which changes the DNA

structure of the white cell, destroys it and thereby weakens the immune system. Having *exploited* the victim, the reproduced cell goes in search of other victims, with the end result of death from the body's lack of a responsive immune system to ward off other diseases, such as pneumonia.

Sin, understood as a state of unbelief, in which this state enters the victim's innermost core of being, his or hers intellect, will and spirit. The result of this copulation parallels the invasion of the white cell, as the virus of sin yields a change of desire and behavior that produces evil actions. These actions go forth and hurt other people. Even personal sin becomes relational. Sin hurts not only the sinner, but the real malice is its evil effect on other people and the whole universe.

I'm not condemning the sinner, or the AIDS victim, but I am drawing a comparison to the activity of a dreaded disease to the activity of sin. Both exploit and are deadly to life.

`There are many avenues a person can follow as he or she moseys through life. It is paradoxical that the more one tries to get gusto, because he is only going around once, and eat, drink and be merry for tomorrow we die, the more self defeating life becomes.

A happy life is a successful life. Happiness is not something external, but rather it is one's internal response to external events. How true is Shakespeare's oft repeated quote: "Nothing is good or bad, but thinking makes it so." This inside-out concept is endorsed by all "pop psychologists" in many forms. Viktor Frankl in his landmark book, Man's Search for Meaning, probably said it best; the ultimate freedom is "the ability to choose one's attitude in a given set of circumstances."

Many chose a Christian way of life. As G.K. Chesterton once said: *"The Christian ideal has not been tried and found wanting. It has been found difficult and left untried."* The difficulty is our freedom to chose. Yet at the same time this is what makes us so special, it is our very, very precious freedom.

Sitting in the bathroom with *Cock Wild* and beating off to the images of anal intercourse and cock sucking doesn't liberate, rather it enslaves a person to his own body in total isolation. Don't believe it? Just let somebody knock on the door while you are so engrossed, see how open to others you might be.

The Christian way of life, is a life of faith. Faith is an attitude that says: "I believe there is a loving God and I believe what he says is true. I also believe he has the power to do what he says and that he'll do it." With this mind-set, we align ourselves, our lives to living now for the kingdom of God that is and yet is not-yet. The kingdom of oneness with God is both now and yet to be completed. We live this life by means of choosing the free gift of God's love and through this gift we are able to obey and serve by applying the power of the cross, the plus sign (+) to the negative (-) events of our circumstances, the people we meet, conditions of work and temptations to evil.

Probably never thought of getting off on the Bible. It's true that a self-induced orgasm can be ecstasy, it is also true that Spiritual penetration can create ecstasy without guilt. Listen to Paul:

> "The word of God is alive and active, sharper than any double-edged sword. It cuts all the way through, to where soul and spirit meet, to where joints and

marrow come together. It judges the desires and thoughts of man's heart"(Hebrews 4:12).

Reading the same passages over and over creates new thoughts and insights about God, others my dick and myself. It's not a head-trip (and here I don't mean head, like in giving head), but a journey of the heart. It's not the ability to spout quotations or give learned view or commentaries. It's not even the boast of reading the Bible from cover to cover. Rather the Bible is a prayer book of faith and love, where the Spirit enters us.

JOHN

As I doodle on a piece of poster board, I fantasize many sizes and shapes of stiff dicks. The triumvirate of me sucking cock while spreading my cheeks and allowing a stiff penis penetrating me to my prostate and at the same time shoving my own steaming prick up a well lubed asshole fills me with wonder. Is it a distortion? My imagination can expand further into a drawing of the consummate sexual activity of a male doing the triangle and with his free hands, jacking off two other men while the sixth male sucks his balls.

So how do we deal with these images of distorted sexuality? We can try harder not to, not to grab my dick, not to look at porn, try harder not to get harder. That's the "either/or" approach. Either I masturbate, or I don't

We can just say "fuck it", and do as we please without any regard to morality, or we can adopted the "both/and" mind-set that takes a realistic, gentler approach to where we are at right now in our sexual and life journey. Sex is so bound up with life and life is bound up with spirituality. Let us celebrate life, sexuality, God, others and ourselves in a synergy of love. Let the light shine in and let sexuality bask in this light of ourselves and otherness, let

love expand with gentle, patience kindness. Understanding the heat of passion, we choose self-control, discipline and realize that rampant, unchecked lust leads us to exploitation, distortion and living a lie. We set our horizon on what the Creator has in mind and has planned for us in the oneness of his kingdom. We strive for unity, harmony and balance, realizing that we go to extremes, but conscious of our distortion, we turn again to the truth of our being and gently forgive ourselves with renewed hope and love.

Late have I loved you, O Beauty ever ancient, ever new, late have I loved you! ... Created things kept me from you, yet if they had not been in you they would not have been at all. You called, you shouted, and you broke through my deafness. You flashed, you shone, and you dispelled my blindness. You breathed your fragrance on me; I drew in breath and now I pant for you. I have tasted you, now I hunger and thirst for more. You touched me, and I burned for your peace.

From the Confessions of
Saint Augustine, bishop

About the Author

About Mr. Mo and the author, Barnabus Fuller. The former is the main character and the later a pseudonym, or pen name. Obviously, neither person will show up for a book signing. Mr. Mo did attend graduate school, received a MRE and undergraduate BA in Philosophy. This enabled him to have a lifetime of 40 different jobs. He is now a man of leisure.

Printed in the United States
82196LV00005B/138